MANOR HOUSES AND CASTLES OF SWEDEN

Drottningholm Castle.

Chinese Pavilion, Drottningholm.

MANOR HOUSES AND CASTLES OF SWEDEN

A Voyage through Five Centuries

Text by
Maita di Niscemi

Preface by
John Train

Introduction by
Ralph Edenheim

Photographs by
Nicolas Sapieha
Francesco Venturi

ANTIQUE COLLECTORS' CLUB

This book was made possible with the help and advice from:

Roland Pålsson,	former Director-General, the Central Board of National Antiquities
Göran Alm,	Curator of the Royal Collections
Lena Daun,	The Swedish Institute, Stockholm
John W. Walldén,	Swedish Information Service, New York
Börje Bengtsson,	Editor-in-Chief of Sköna Hem

We thank Charlotte Bonnier for her continuous encouragement; Catharina von Schinkel for her unfailing assistance; all the owners, Curators, and Directors of the castles and manor houses included in this book, for their interest, kind help and hospitality.

We thank Ralph Edenheim for the thoughtful and generous advice given to this project since its inception.

All reproductions of prints have been supplied by **the Department of Maps and Prints, Uppsala University Library.** The areal photographs have kindly been lent by **Lantmäteriet, Gävle.**

The photographs on pages 22 to 35 and 53 to 55, by Peo Eriksson, have been kindly provided by **Sköna Hem.**
The photograph on page 21, is courtesy of the **Royal Collection.**
The photographs of Trolleholm have been kindly provided by Gustaf Trolle-Bonde.
The photographs on pages 70, 166 and 201 are by Ralph Edenheim.

Project directed by	**M. T. Train.**
Production by	**José Brandão.**

Design by A. Milani.
Color separation by Grafiseis.
Printed by Printer Portuguesa.
Copyright © 1988 M. T. Train-Scala Books, New York.
Photographs © 1988 Kea.

Distributed in Great Britain by:

Antique Collectors' Club
5 Church Street
Woodbridge, Suffolk, IP12 1DS, United Kingdom

Published in Sweden by **Legenda.**

Distributed in the United States by:
Harper & Row, Publishers, Inc.
10 E 53 St., New York, NY 10022.

ISBN 1 85149 080 9
LC 87 960276

CONTENTS

FOREWORD 6
INTRODUCTION 9

STOCKHOLM AND ITS COAST

Royal Palace 14
Drottningholm 16
Kina Pavilion 22
Haga 30
Ulriksdal 36
Rosendal 38
Tyresö 44
Sandemar 46
Beatelund 50

SVEALAND

Gripsholm 52
Sturehof 60
Hörningsholm 63
Tullgarn 64
Thureholm 70
Elghammar 72
Åkerö 78
Ericsberg 86
Biby 88
Stora Sundby 90
Strömsholm 92
Bystad 94
Tidö 98
Fullerö 106
Engsö 108
Grönsöö 111

NORTH OF STOCKHOLM

Rydboholm 112
Rosersberg 116
Steninge 122
Skokloster 126
Hammarby 132

Salsta 134
Österby and Leufsta 136
Örbyhus 140

GÖTALAND

Sturefors 144
Adelsnäs 150
Vadstena 152
Koberg 154
Lackö 160
Mariedal 165
Gripenberg 166
Kalmar 167
Borgholm 172

SKÅNE

Krapperup 174
Svenstorp 177
Trolleholm 178
Marsvinsholm 183
Wrams Gunnarstorp 184
Krageholm 186
Svaneholm 188
Sövdeborg 190
Torup 194
Övedskloster 198
Glimmingehus 204
Kronovall 206
Trolle-Ljungby 208
Vittskövle 211
Wanås 214

BIBLIOGRAPHY 216

FOREWORD

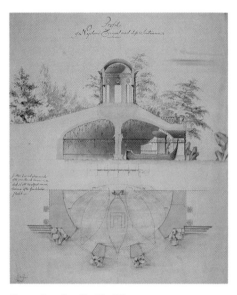

Drawing by F. M. Piper
for Neptune Temple
at Haga.

From earliest history the Swedes have been a single race, never successfully invaded, thanks in part to the extreme rigor of their winter climate. Tacitus refers to the Suiones, or Svear, living near present-day Stockholm. To the south dwelt Goths, whence Gotland. "Beowulf" describes their wars, in which the Goths were eventually overcome by the Svear, who gave their name to Sweden. The southern tip of the Swedish peninsula—today's Skåne—was called by the Romans Scania, whence Scandinavia.

The word Viking covers both the Swedes and their Norwegian and Danish cousins—as do Norse and Norman: "north-man." The Vikings were sea-raiders like none in history before or since. Heading west across the Atlantic they mercilessly harried the British Isles. They settled Iceland, and established a community in Newfoundland: both were much warmer then. The long Viking ships penetrated the rivers of Russia, whose name, indeed, refers to the Rus—the red-faced and fair-haired invaders. The descendants of their chief, Rurik, ruled there for seven hundred years. The Vikings even passed on through the Black Sea to Byzantium and Greece.

These dauntless sea-rovers eventually established themselves in northwestern France and on the British coast. Indeed, when William the Conqueror defeated Harold of England at Hastings in 1066, it was only a question of *which* Scandinavian would triumph: William and his Normans were Norse, but so, as his name implied, was Harold. And only weeks before, Harold's army had repelled an invasion by yet another Norseman, Harold Hardrader, who had sailed over from Norway.

The Normans then pushed into the Mediterranean. For centuries they dominated Sicily, whose Norman-Arab style is one of the most singular achievements of world architecture.

Christian missionaries reached Sweden in the ninth century. It was hoped—vainly—that their message of love and peace might inhibit the dreadful scourge of Viking raids on the coasts of Europe. In the fourteenth century St. Birgitta's revelations stirred Christians everywhere; the Order she founded spread widely, and prospers to this day.

When Gustav Vasa, having driven the Danes out of the country, became autocratic ruler of Sweden, he realized that he could replenish his exhausted treasury by following the example of his contemporary Henry VIII in appropriating the wealth of the church. So he broke away from Rome—an act not displeasing to his independently-minded people—declared for the radical new ideas of Lutheranism, created a new Swedish state religion, and transferred to the state the rich bishoprics and conventual properties of the Roman Church. The Pope raged, but was far away.

The Thirty Years' War, pitting Catholics against Protestants throughout Europe, found Gustav's grandson, Gustav II Adolf, on the throne. A brilliant soldier, he led the Protestant alliance combatting the Hapsburg forces of the Holy Roman Empire, led by their formidable captain, Wallenstein. In this war of religion Richelieu, prodded by his wily "éminence grise," Père Joseph, cynically placed the wealth of Catholic France behind Protestant Sweden in the hope of humbling France's fellow-Catholic Hapsburg rivals. Gustav II Adolf reduced one German city after another, finally capturing Munich in 1632. He was killed in an assault on Wallenstein's camp later that year, but his nephew, Karl Gustav, had reached Prague when the Treaty of Westfalia was concluded in 1648. Munich . . . Prague! These are capitals vastly distant from Stockholm. During this period Sweden also threw out its first colony in the New World since the Vikings: New Sweden, on the Delaware River, eventually taken over by the Dutch.

Elghammar, the library.

In the eighteenth century began a golden age of Swedish culture, including the founding of the Academy by Queen Lovisa Ulrika, and a flowering of writers, artists, scientists and architects. I will not go further here into that splendid period, since essentially it is the subject of this book.

How did it come about that this ferociously military race became the prudent neutralists of today? A lust for heroic mention in the history books, with equestrian statues in the public parks, is more the obsession of an individual than a people. Indeed, the price of military glory for one is usually misery for many: both for the soldiers, felled by disease or wounds, and for the simple folk at home, ravaged by invading columns or taxed remorselessly to pay for armies in distant fields.

So by 1800 Sweden was ready to sheathe the sword. The debilitated successors of Gustav II Adolf had fallen on sad times. Their conquests had been wrested from them, and the population was restless to the point of anarchy. (Count Axel Fersen, Marie Antoinette's gallant admirer, was pulled from his carriage, tortured and killed by a mob during a royal funeral procession without receiving any assistance from the participating troops.)

In 1810, the position of crown prince—succeeding to the throne after the death of the figurehead Karl XIII—was offered to Napoleon's Marshal Bernadotte. This was heady stuff for the former

Gripsholm Castle.

sergeant from Pau, who accepted with satisfaction. Firmly grasping his powers, the new prince promptly made alliances with Napoleon's enemies Russia and Britain. He then profited from France's weakness to attack its ally, Denmark, and detach Norway, which became united with Sweden under the same king until its independence a century later.

After that, however, Bernadotte, who became King Karl XIV Johan, declared an end to foreign adventures. Instead, for a century and a half Sweden has, in spite of many challenges, followed a course of heavily armed neutrality, avoiding involvement in any war. The energy and money that was once directed abroad has instead turned inward, to the extensive social engineering and industrial development for which the country has in recent generations been distinguished.

I touched at the outset on the fearful Swedish winter, which, indeed, has had many effects on the architecture depicted in these pages. The camera of one of this book's photographers actually froze during work on one of the snow scenes . . . understandably few. Those dark winters produce a hunger for the sun that becomes an obsession. I was related by marriage to a Swedish lady of limited means. She pre-paid her own funeral, in order that when she died she would not become a burden on her family. But during one terrible winter she could stand it no more, and sold her funeral back to the company to raise money for a trip to Italy. Off she went. She enjoyed a brief time of bliss in the warm southern sun, but then, far from home, she died, and did indeed become a burden on the family. But the family understood perfectly. Every Swede would.

John Train

INTRODUCTION

During the late Middle Ages, the rising nobility built Sweden's monumental manors. Thereafter, palaces and manors continued to be built through five centuries of changing history. During the Renaissance, the Vasa kings and the ever more powerful nobles competed with one another to achieve the heights of magnificence, recruiting foreign architects, artists, and craftsmen who introduced the latest styles from the European capitals. The nobility's power and wealth were further manifested in the many large stone houses built during the early seventeenth century. After the Peace at Westphalia in 1648, construction reached its peak and the royal family, gentry, and returning military commanders built palaces of a grandeur unequaled elsewhere in Europe. During the reign of Karl XII (1697-1718), thanks to the expense and ravages of war, the days of glory passed away; thereafter the devastated land was slowly rebuilt with the help of Swedish architects, who were trained mainly in France and Italy. It was they who, at midcentury, created the Swedish rococo manor house, which became the ideal building of the "Period of Liberty" and left its mark on Sweden's domestic architecture for a long time.

View from Tyresö garden

During the nineteenth century, the building of palaces and manor houses reached its climax. Powerful landowners, successful entrepreneurs, and prosperous merchants built and rebuilt palaces and manors to an unprecedented extent. They borrowed freely from history's stylistic inventory and used their great wealth to create exciting though not always beautiful settings.

Before all this magnificence came into being—that is, in the Middle Ages—the home of a Swedish nobleman did not differ greatly from that of a farmer, generally consisting of a timbered two room house. The homes of the gentry, of course, tended to be somewhat larger and more ornate than those of the farmers; they were, in addition, often surrounded by a defensive palisade, or a wall and a tower. By the late Middle Ages, however, the defense and dwelling functions had become united, giving rise to tall stone houses, often with projecting corner towers (Vikshus, Örbyhus) and surrounded by ramparts and moats (Glimmingehus).

King Gustav Vasa was among the first to construct a castle in the common sense of the word—that is, a stone house with one or more corner or central towers. The best example is Gripsholm, but that type was soon succeeded by the edifices of the aristocracy (Penningby, Stora Sundby, Hörningsholm). The European Renaissance came to Sweden

Strömsholm Castle

Turkish tent at Drottningholm.

with King Gustav Vasa's sons. With the help of imported building contractors, they rebuilt Stockholm's old Three Crowns Palace as well as the palaces in Kalmar and Vadstena in a magnificent Renaissance style, with elegant details based on engravings by Sebastiano Serlio, the Italian architectural theorist. During the same period, in Scania, now the southernmost province of Sweden, noblemen built stately establishments comprising either one large stone house (Svenstorp) or adjacent houses with ornamented gables and sometimes tall, diagonally placed towers (Skarhult, Svaneholm, Torup, Vittskövle). At that time Scania belonged to Denmark and was that country's richest province. In Sweden proper, as opposed to Scania, stone buildings were not as common during the Renaissance, although some noteworthy dwellings were erected at this time. It was Chancellor Axel Oxenstierna, with the assistance of the architect Simon de la Vallée, who built Filholm and Tidö. Both are brilliant examples of the French-Dutch Renaissance style.

With Simon de la Vallée, a renowned family of architects appeared on the Swedish scene. He and his son Jean put their mark on the late-Renaissance and early-baroque style. The House of the Nobility in Stockholm stands today as the principal example of Simon's work, while Jean created a number of palaces and manors, the most remarkable of which are Karlberg, Venngarn, Mariedal, and Runsa. Both Simon and Jean collaborated with another immigrant architect, Nicodemus Tessin the Elder, the most prominent member of the second largest and perhaps most famous family of architects in Sweden. He, his son Nicodemus Tessin the Younger, and his grandson Carl Gustav would for a century take the lead in Swedish architecture.

The Peace of Westphalia had made Sweden a great power, a fact reflected in the unprecedented grandeur of Swedish buildings. Many of the large stone houses built during the early seventeenth century were now extended and embellished with lavish ornamentation (Nynäs, Ericsberg, Karlberg, Läckö). Others were newly built on the same grand scale and in a similarly rich configuration (Salsta, Sjöö, Skokloster, Mariedal, Steninge). First in the line of noble builders was Queen Kristina's favorite, Count Magnus Gabriel De la Gardie, who later became chancellor.

In the architectural competition between the royal family and the nobility, Queen Hedvig Eleonora came out the winner. During her long period as queen dowager (1660-1715), she probably did more building in Sweden than anyone else before or since. Drottningholm became so large and was so lavishly adorned that it surpassed Versailles at that time. Strömsholm was built as a grandiose set in a beautiful park; never furnished during the queen's time, it was built to be the subject of splendid illustration in Erik Dahlbergh's large collection of engravings, the *Svecia Antiqua et Hodierna*, along with a great many other palaces and manors. (Many had not yet been built at the time they were drawn and others were made to look grander than they actually were, all for the noble purpose of showing off, to an amazed Europe, Sweden's glory and magnificence.) When Stockholm's palace burned down in 1697, Nicodemus Tessin the Younger was given the opportunity to build a majestic new royal palace in the European spirit. Well prepared after his studies in France and Italy, Tessin went to work immediately. Italy, above all, provided the inspiration for the new palace's façades, porticoes, and stairwells.

At the beginning of the eighteenth century, while both King Karl XII and the nobles were at war with Russia, a powerful woman became Sweden's architectural standard bearer as the Carolinian era passed into history. Christina Törnflyckt, the wife of Count Carl Piper, a royal councilor, consolidated and built rich holdings on a grandiose scale. Before her husband became a prisoner of the Russians (after the battle of Poltava in 1709), he had begun Sturefors, which was completed largely along the lines specified by Nicodemus Tessin the Younger. Tessin was also of help to the countess when Krageholm, a Renaissance castle that had been damaged by fire, was rebuilt as a Carolinian palace. The stairwell and beautiful palace chapel are directly attributable to him. Later in her long life, the countess also built Christinehof and, in the 1740s, rebuilt the original medieval Engsö, which she enlarged. As already noted, the military exploits of Karl XII proved disastrous to Sweden. Hence when peace finally came in about 1720, there was little building activity. Among the notable exceptions were Tullgarn, built by the chancellor, Count Magnus Julius De la Gardie; Björksund, built by the county governor, Count Nils Gyllenstierna; and Bergshammar, built by the courtier Baron Johan Gabriel Sack. They all used the same architect, Joseph Gabriel Destain, who had immigrated from France. All of these buildings reflect the austerity of the Carolinian period. In Bergshammar's design, however, the earliest hints of Swedish rococo are evident.

Since the building of the Stockholm Palace had almost ceased during Karl XII's lifetime, Tessin did not live to see his life work completed. The project therefore passed into the hands of his son, Carl Gustav. He, however, was above all an architectural theorist, connoisseur of the arts, and politician; he therefore left the palace project to Carl Hårleman, who became the greatest architect of Sweden's Period of Liberty. Hårleman designed and built a number of impressive interiors, but he died prematurely and failed to complete the project, which was taken over by Carl Johan Cronstedt and Jean Eric Rehn. It can be said that these three architects shaped Swedish rococo. Hårleman was well prepared for his task, having pursued lengthy studies in France and Italy, where he sketched classical monuments and copied the plans of contemporary buildings. Following French patterns, he created the typical rococo manor, its most idealistic shape

Courtyard at Tidö

is evident in Åkerö, which Hårleman designed for Carl Gustav Tessin, the eighteenth century's greatest cultural personality. Other brilliant examples are Svindersvik and Övedskloster.

Another queen who left her mark on Swedish architecture was Lovisa Ulrika, sister of Frederick the Great of Prussia, who took a strong interest in science, art, and theater. At her initiative, Drottningholm Palace was remodeled; the famous Drottningholm Theater, one of Europe's best-preserved rococo theaters, was built; and Kina Pavilion, in the park around Drottningholm, was created. Kina Pavilion is an example of another facet of rococo. In Sweden as elsewhere in Europe, there was much interest in the exotic, in particular the Chinese. This was expressed in pavilions and gazebos (Grönsöö), royal summer residences, and—perhaps most importantly—the interiors of traditionally designed manors (as at Sturefors). Carl Johan Cronstedt, though not notable as an architect, won a place in history as the creator of a different example of Swedish rococo: the tiled stove. In the artistic design of stoves, however, he was surpassed by his colleagues Jean Eric Rehn and Carl Fredrik Adelcrantz. The latter, who had built both the Drottningholm Theater and the Kina Pavilion, drafted Sturehov for Baron Johan Liljecrantz, Gustav III's finance minister in about 1770. Liljecrantz was part owner of Marieberg, the eighteenth century's most successful artistic faïence and porcelain factory, famous for its wide range of brilliant colors. As a result, the rooms at Sturehov were furnished with gracefully fashioned tiled stoves from Marieberg. Jean Eric Rehn became famous for many elegant interiors, among them Queen Lovisa Ulrika's library at Drottningholm and the parade rooms at Sturefors and Övedskloster. He is also credited with many stately manors in their entirety: Erstavik, which was built for the president of the East India Company, Herman Petersen; Ljung, of which the chancellor, the elder Count Axel von Fersen, was proprietor; and Lambohov, built for Baron Carl Fredrik Sinclair. Jean Eric Rehn was also a designer of silver and faience and a valued drawing teacher to the future King Gustav III. Rehn finally forged the link between the rococo and the subsequent Gustavian style.

After Gustav III succeeded to the throne, a vital period of building began; this took a turn toward the classical after the king's journey to Italy from 1783 to 1784. "The King's Pavilion" at Haga perhaps best captures the elegant spirit of the era, and the theater that Gustav III had created at Gripsholm clearly reflects the classical tendency. Certain other manors from the Gustavian period deserve mention as well: the graceful Heby, which well represents Gustavian manors in general; the more austere, classicist Hylinge: and the genuinely neo-classical Elghammar, which is quite unique in Swedish architecture. During the Gustavian period, trade flourished and there was lively building activity around the Swedish iron works, especially in the Uppland province. Whole communities were shaped in a spirit of uniformity, with the manor as a center of each. Now came Gimo and Forsmark, designed by Jean Eric Rehn, while Harg and Österby were created by a less known builder, Elias Kessler. By the 1720s, Leufsta had already been built, but Rehn was commissioned to redo the interiors in the main building and to develop the famous library and nature pavilions.

Detail of wall painting at Åkerö

The neoclassic style took a more austere form and, of course, showed a stronger French influence when the French Marshal Jean Baptiste Bernadotte became Sweden's King Karl XIV Johan. Rosendal, his summer residence at Djurgården, typifies this epoch. The enormous porphyry vase in its garden was manufactured at Älvdalen's porphyry works, which the king owned. Porphyry became extremely popular and is still often seen, sometimes in imitation form, in interiors, especially in handicraft objects. Rosendal, designed by Fredrik Blom, was probably the first "prefabricated" building in Sweden. Blom made a number of prefabricated houses, some of which were exported. Examples of the decorative art from Karl Johan's period include a number of interiors in the older Rosersberg Palace.

The last great period of palace and manor building in Sweden began at the turn of the nineteenth century. In creating these historic structures, the royal family and the nobility now met competition from successful entrepreneurs and prosperous merchants. With the help of several architects, a burgeoning building industry, and many skilled craftsmen, palaces and manors were built and rebuilt in all historical styles. A Norman knight's stronghold (Stora Sundby), a southern French Renaissance fortress (Trolleholm), a Vasa castle (Koberg), a Dutch (Wrams Gunnarstorp) or French baroque palace (Kronovall), an English country house (Adelsnäs)—all were created with the same happy imagination and technical proficiency. These buildings offer a quick and lively recapitulation of Sweden's and Europe's architectural history. Much of what had been left unfinished or undecorated was now restored, supplemented, or completed.

Detail of intarsio work at Kalmar

Ralph Edenheim

THE ROYAL PALACE

The north-west facade of Stockholm's
Royal Palace, the largest royal residence
in Scandinavia. It was completed to the
designs of Nicodemus Tessin the
Younger after the preceding building
was destroyed by a fire in 1697.

Stockholm's Royal Palace, the Swedish capital's most important building, stands on an embankment above the spot where fresh inland waters meet the brackish waves of the Baltic Sea. The present structure was designed in 1697, the old Three Crowns Palace having burned in the spring of that year, as king Karl XI lay in state. The new king, Karl XII (1682-1718), his grandmother Queen Hedvig Eleonora (1636-1715), and their architect Nicodemus Tessin the Younger (1654-1728) worked together on the building of the new palace. From far away battlefields, the monarch (who was more a fighter than a builder) would send home instructions to be filtered through the old queen's long experience and Tessin's foreign training. Although later rulers and their architects left their marks on this 600-room structure, the palace stands today as a monument to all three: Lorenzo Bernini's former student, a great lady who was also a great builder, and Sweden's last warrior king. The palace, in addition to its decorative riches—including magnificent tapestries and a silver throne given to Queen Kristina by Magnus Gabriel De la Gardie—contains several museums, the most important being the Royal Armory, in which the lives of past monarchs are recorded. Here are displayed the hat and uniform worn by Karl XII when he was shot in 1718 at Fredrikshald, Norway, and the costume that Gustav III wore to the masked ball at the Stockholm Opera on March 16, 1792, during which he was wounded. He was then carried to the palace, where he died on March 29 of the same year.

Tessin planned to recreate northern Stockholm around his masterpiece. But the funds required for this great project were devoured by Karl XII's wars. Even the construction of the central building was suspended after the Swedish defeat at Poltava in 1709. What we have today is the palace, the review square, the church (rebuilt by Johan Eberhard Carlberg following Tessin's specifications), the north bridge, and Tessin's own magnificent italianate house with its triangular garden to the south of the palace. Here, as in the royal building, we see how very much Tessin was influenced by the Rome of the Farnese popes. Although the mansion is not very large, it is monumentaly conceived and its garden reveals Tessin's great ingenuity in creating trompe l'oeil perspectives. Tessin's design for the Royal Palace greatly influenced his fellow architects. A child of the Italian baroque, inspired by the Rome of Sixtus V, Tessin helped to turn the eighteenth century into the "Roman era" of northern European architecture.

The interior of Stockholm's palace, the largest royal structure in Scandinavia, completes the impression of imperial strength and power that Tessin and his collaborators built into the façade, which is partially based on that of the Villa Farnese. But the decorations of the state apartments owe a great debt to the France of Louis XIV. The gallery of Karl XI that was begun before the fire is largely inspired by the Salon de la Guerre and the Gallerie des Glaces of Versailles. Here literally hundreds can dine seated beneath the allegorical paintings Jacques Foucquet completed in 1702. Throne and Reception rooms bear the names of succeeding monarchs but the spirit of the palace remains that of an era when all Europe strove in emulation of Le Roi Soleil, and Karl XII, dazzled by French power, dreamed of a firmly established Baltic empire and an ever expanding Swedish hegemony.

DROTTNINGHOLM PALACE

Aerial view of Drottningholm Palace. Nicodemus Tessin the Elder began building the palace for Queen Hedvig Eleonora in 1662, it was completed in 1681. The design is of French inspiration and it is often refered to as the Versaille of the North. The gardens were designed by Nicodemus Tessin the Younger, in the early eighteenth century, in the style of Le Nôtre, and have been perfectly restored.

Opposite page:
Detail of one of the two entrance gates to Drottningholm garden showing the initials of Queen Hedvig Eleonora. The gates were installed in 1697 by Johan Hårleman.

Today the official residence of Sweden's royal family is Drottningholm Palace, "The Queen's Island." Standing beside Lake Mälaren, this two-hundred-room building is a monument to two extraordinary royal ladies.

The first, Queen Hedvig Eleonora of Holstein-Gottorp (1636-1715), was one of the great builders of the seventeenth century. A bride at eighteen and a widow at twenty-four, she survived both her husband, Karl X, and her son, Karl XI. She saw the apogee of Sweden's Baltic empire and died the year her grandson, Karl XII, returned from Turkey.

Hedvig Eleonora, whose initials are woven into the palace's main gates, was never much involved in national politics. Fate made her a

regent—first for her son, then for her grandson—but her true interests lay in domestic life and in those forms of architecture that she considered complementary to her style of living. She built, rebuilt, and inhabited castles throughout the land. These were usually on or near crown properties. Drottningholm was an exception.

Hedvig Eleonora had bought the palace from the widow of Magnus Gabriel De la Gardie in 1661, but it burned down the following year. Thereupon the queen asked Nicodemus Tessin the Elder to create an entirely new structure for the site. Soon he had completed the plans for a palace reminiscent of France's Vaux-le-Vicomte, and the shell was constructed by 1664. It looked very like the present structure except that it was pink with gray trim and was surmounted by a high tower supporting a huge, gilded royal crown. This tower proved dangerous and was later pulled down.

Those who insist on seeing in Drottningholm "the Versailles of Sweden" will find support in the sweeping staircase and the two large commemorative galleries. The upper gallery is hung with paintings illustrating the battles of Karl XI, while the lower one is devoted to the exploits of Karl X. The latter is more historically interesting. The paintings here are winter scenes, showing seventeenth-century battles and bivouacs. Of prime interest are those commemorating Karl X's greatest exploit, the thirty-kilometer crossing, on foot, of "the Great Belt," the rarely frozen channel between Sjalland and Jylland in Denmark. At the beginning of February 1658, Eric Dahlbergh, a young officer of the engineering corps, reconnoitered the ice on horseback at peril of his life. Dahlbergh assured the king that the ice would hold, and it did. Five thousand men with guns and wagons crossed from Svendborg to Langeland to Lolland to Falster, meeting no resistance. On February 11, as the ice began to melt, the king was in Vordingborg. Erik Dahlbergh lived to provide Johan Philip Lemke with the sketches that became the basis for these paintings and to become famous for his own books of engravings, *Svecia Antiqua et Hodierna*, depicting Swedish homes of the late seventeenth century as their owners wished them to be seen. A portrait of Dahlbergh as an older man hangs in an anteroom in Drottningholm today.

French baroque influence is also evident in the state bedroom of Hedvig Eleonora. Originally designed in 1668 by Tessin the Elder, it was even more ostentatious and heavy—with its columns, railings,

Drottningholm Palace.
Originally planned as a picture gallery,
in 1760 Queen Lovisa Ulrika
commissioned the architect Jean Eric
Rehn to transform it into a white and
gold library.

swatches of fabric, and numerous cherubim—than it is today. For more than forty years, it was painted black and gold in mourning for the late king.

Although she received visits in this, her official bedroom, Hedvig Eleonora actually slept in a simple stuccoed chamber that is now part of the royal private apartments. The elaborate state bedroom did not actually become a sleeping chamber until Lovisa Ulrika of Brandenburg, a younger sister of Frederick the Great of Prussia, moved into the palace. She received Drottningholm as a wedding present on her marriage in 1744 to Crown Prince Adolf Fredrik and spent many years improving both it and the park. She slept, whenever she was in the residence, in the queen's state bedroom.

Lovisa Ulrika was "fair as day itself" and clever as well. She corresponded with learned men and women in several languages and had a gold and white library installed at the palace. It is considered by many to be Sweden's most beautiful room. Here she received the great Swedish naturalist Carolus Linnaeus.

The library houses signed first editions of Voltaire's works, along with well-thumbed volumes in Latin, Italian, French, English, and Swedish. Jean Erik Rehn created the library's decorations. The desk and book ladder were made by George Haupt, the court cabinetmaker.

In 1753, two years after Adolf Fredrik had succeeded to the throne, Lovisa Ulrika introduced theatricals in a makeshift theater at Ulriksdal palace. When this structure burned down in 1762, the queen commissioned Carl Fredrik Adelcrantz to build a bigger and better theater at Drottningholm. This theater is still in operation today, as are its eighteenth-century sets for *Cosi Fan Tutte* and *The Magic Flute*. The scenery is maneuvered by hand, as it always has been, and the singers and actors retire between the acts to the handsome dressing rooms—complete with day beds—that the queen provided for them over two hundred years ago.

Queen Lovisa Ulrika was both extravagant and ambitious. From the moment she arrived in Sweden, she schemed in favor of absolute monarchy—at the expense of both friends and counselors. Even an abortive coup in 1756, which brought death to several of her supporters, could not stop her. Throughout her life, Prussian autocracy remained to her the norm and her brother its ideal embodiment. It is

sad to note that when, as a widow, she at last visited Berlin for the first time since her marriage, she remarked that Berlin seemed somehow dull without Voltaire. Frederick the Great replied that he had been noticing this same fact for the last sixteen years.

DROTTNINGHOLM: KINA PAVILION

July 24, 1753, was Queen Lovisa Ulrika's thirty-third birthday. In an age when women were considered old at thirty, this might have been a rather grim occasion; instead, it was a day of sheer enchantment. In the morning the learned queen inaugurated the Swedish Academy of Learning, History, and Antiquity, in emulation of similar institutions already established in Paris and Berlin. After theatricals in the Great Hall, King Adolf Fredrik, who had been secretive for several weeks, suggested a drive through Drottningholm's formal gardens. Riding through avenues of trees and around the parterre laid out by Nicodemus Tessin the Younger, the couple reached an oak grove near the lake. Here, on a gentle rise, they discovered a brand new fairytale palace: a Chinese pavilion built in sections at the arsenal in Stockholm and shipped by night in barges to be secretly assembled in this secluded corner of the palace grounds. In front of the pink, green, and ochre birthday pavilion, the corps of cadets, dressed in Chinese costumes, performed supposedly Chinese exercises while their band played "Oriental" music. Then, under the indulgent gaze of the king (who had engineered the whole project), a tiny mandarin stepped forward to offer the queen the gilded keys to the pavilion and an inventory of its contents. His eyes cast down, the child pronounced a greeting in a strange-sounding language. At first, as Lovisa Ulrika later wrote her mother in Berlin, the queen did not realize that she was being addressed by the seven-year-old crown prince, the future Gustav III. But when he looked up at her with his light-blue Brandenburg eyes, she recognized and embraced her eldest son. Then the royal family entered the pavilion to examine the queen's gifts.

These presents are known to us from the inventory of 1777. They included the pavilion's furnishings and Hedvig Eleonora's splendid collection of white china as well as other Chinese porcelains from the early seventeenth century.

Two operas were performed at Drottningholm that night, the ball lasted until six in the morning, and the festivities went on for eight days. Kina could not have been more sumptuously launched—or better received.

Adolf Fredrik and his family so loved Kina that, when the original wood structure began showing signs of age, Carl Fredrik Adelcrantz was asked to design a larger, permanent version in stone. The work

A separate dining wing on the side of the Chinese Pavilion still houses an eighteenth-century mechanical table that can be raised and lowered to the cellar to assure perfect privacy.

The Chinese Pavilion at Drottningholm.
The Green Salon of the pavilion was the gathering place of the court. The queen and her ladies in waiting would work on their embroidery while the gentlemen played games of chance. The room's decor was inspired by the French painter François Boucher. The stools are eighteenth-century originals while the papier-mâché Chinese dolls in the niches are nineteenth-century reproductions.

One of the papier-mâché dolls, almost one meter high.

The Chinese Pavilion at Drottningholm.
The Yellow Cabinet, designed by Carl Fredrik Adelcrantz exemplifies the strong influence of William Chamber, a leading authority on eighteenth-century interior design. It is paneled in Chinese lacquer.

began in 1763 and the building we know today was soon completed. This northernmost example of the eighteenth-century rage for chinoiserie is by no means a work inspired entirely by China. The entrance hall, paved and decorated with European marbles, could be that of a French rococo chateau. The Mirror Room directly behind it is also a classic example of mid-eighteenth-century restraint and elegance. The exoticism begins with the Chinese lacquer panels in the Red Cabinet (to the left of the Marble Hall). The decorations of this and the Yellow Cabinet on the opposite side of the hallway are taken from a volume entitled *Designs of Chinese Buildings, Furniture, etc.,* which was published in London by the Swedish-born architect William Chambers, while the "Chinese" scenes painted on the walls of the Green Salon and the Blue Lounge are variations on paintings by Watteau and Boucher.

Although the royal family never passed the night in Kina Pavilion, they spent a good deal of time there. The king had a carpentry shop in the east wing, where he could putter to his heart's content, while elsewhere the queen and her ladies worked at wall panels for the aptly named Embroidered Room. The fire screen in the Mirror Room, a hanging Chinese flower basket, was created by Princess Sofia Albertina. Upstairs, the Octagonal Room is still decorated with imaginary landscapes executed in sepia tones by Lovisa Ulrika and the crown prince in 1763. Behind the Octagonal Room, the Oval Room (once Gustav III's study) looks out upon a sea of trees. Here, both as prince and king, Gustav dreamed, studied, and planned for a great reign and the buildings that would embody his concept of monarchy.

The entrance hall between the yellow and red cabinets has a polycrome marble floor. The wall decorations were inspired by William Chamber's book, "Design of Chinese Buildings," published in London in 1757.

Although Gustav III liked to improve every palace in which he might reside, he always hungered for something uniquely his own. But Drottningholm and Kina bore the stamp of Lovisa Ulrika. In 1778, after a bitter quarrel over her grandson's paternity, the widowed queen was forbidden to enter the palace or its theater; but her spirit remained everywhere. Therefore, as the years passed, Gustav III started thinking about creating buildings that would be completely his own; even so, Kina was always close to his heart. On the days that the king felt free to entertain his intimates at Kina, a playing card—the king of hearts—was tacked on the door of the anteroom of Drottningholm Palace. When duty prevailed and the king had to receive the full court or foreign delegations at the palace, the card affixed to the door was the king of spades.

Gustav III loved the theater. As a young man, he had helped inaugurate his mother's theater at Drottningholm with a recitation from *Iphigenia at Tauris.* Later, as king, he eagerly performed at every opportunity, in Swedish as well as French. He wrote plays and operas in Swedish, the most famous being *Gustav Vasa;* a didactic and patriotic work that enjoyed great success. Most of the king's theatrical writings amounted to propaganda, in which he rewrote history so as to favor a strong monarchy. (At the age of seven, the future king wrote to his tutor, Count Carl Gustaf Tessin, about the virtues of Camillus as opposed to the shortcomings of Coriolanus.)

Throughout Gustav III's reign, the theater at Drottningholm was active as never before. During one Christmas holiday, the king starred in eight of the twelve plays presented to the assembled nobility. He

The Chinese Pavilion at Drottningholm.
The Sewing Room, decorated with silk embroidery executed by Queen Lovisa Ulrika and her ladies in waiting to designs of Carl Fredrik Adelcrantz. The blanc-de-chine figures flanking the window were part of Queen Hedvig Eleonora's collection.

The Red Cabinet is furnished with eighteenth-century Swedish tables and chairs, Chinese lacquer panels and mirrors, and famille-rose figurines.

The library houses the collection of Queen Hedvig Eleonora, one of the first European collectors to appreciate blanc-de-chine.

A selection of two rare duck statuettes from the Kand Hsis period.

loved his players and spent so much time with them and his scenic designers that both friend and foe reproached him for his theatrical obsession. They did not know the secret of Gustav III's phenomenal memory. He could and did remember for years scripts, documents, and dispatches that he had heard, read, or glanced at only once. The job of memorizing eight plays in a fortnight was as nothing to such a mind. Gustav III also closely followed the construction of many of the sets that are still in storage at Drottningholm. He worked with Fredrik Magnus Piper on plans for a romantic park to be laid out around the formal baroque gardens, and he populated both park and gardens with marble statues brought back from Italy.

As one of his last projects at Drottningholm, Gustav had Louis Jean Desprez, his scenic designer, build a red brick Gothic tower at the end of a tree-lined alleyway. This tower was used only once as an optical telegraph to send birthday greetings to Stockholm on the crown prince's birthday.

Gustav III brought English Chippendale furniture from other palaces to augment the furnishings of Kina. He had Carl Fredrik Adelcrantz design a sumptuous copper tent to shelter his guards from the rain. But by 1781, when the tent was finished, the king, his architects, and his landscape gardener were all thinking in terms of a newly purchased nearby property. Drottningholm and Kina had become the past. In the last years of his life, Gustav III concentrated solely on Haga.

HAGA PAVILION

Bust of Gustav III by Johan Tobias Sergel—1784—in the mirrored Drawing Room at Haga.

Opposite page:
Seen from the lake side, facing the Mirrored Drawing Room, the Haga Pavilion is a masterpiece in the late Gustavian style. Commissioned by Gustav III, it was built by Olof Tempelman in 1788. The surrounding park was designed by Fredrik Magnus Piper.

The Haga Pavilion is among the most beautiful royal residences in Europe and was planned as a "pleasure dome" where the king could reside while awaiting the completion of his vast new neoclassic palace in Haga Park. This projected palace, whose cyclopean ruins lie a short walk from the pavilion, was never completed. The difference in scale between the achieved and dreamed of is truly remarkable.

The pavilion was begun in 1788 by Olof Tempelman. It is small, built for a man seeking isolation from mounting public discontent. In addition to quarters for the king himself, there was permanent accomodation for a valet, who slept in the king's dressing room surrounded by several life-size dummies wearing clothes for Gustav to choose among for the next day. One room was assigned to the crown prince, one to the governor, and one to guests. The king's guards were lodged in copper tents half a mile from the pavilion. The watchmen snoozed in the vestibule, which also served as a pantry, since the real kitchen was in a building across the road. Secretaries working in the king's council chamber wrote at flat tables that pulled out of the window frames.

The pavilion was the embodiment, not just of luxury but, in terms of a royal court, of privacy. Its decorations, planned by Louis Masreliez in the antique style favored by Raphael, are brightly colored and elegant. One wonders what the decorations of Haga Palace might have been like. Actually, we can make a good guess. The drawings executed for Gustav by Louis Jean Desprez, the king's French architect and scenery designer, still exist and show that Gustav was thinking in terms of colonnades, rotundas, and pediments, all of gigantic size, as well as a national pantheon of statues. An idea of the king's preference in statuary can be gleaned from his collection of antiquities, which reflects the prevailing eighteenth-century taste. Comprising one of the first museums of antiquities ever to be open to the public outside of Italy, these objects now repose in the Royal Palace of Stockholm. Here are Greek vases overly restored, Roman copies of Greek statues, cork models of antique temples, Minerva, Apollo, the Nine Muses—and, centerpiece of the collection, a life-sized, supine, sleeping Endymion.

Haga Pavilion was decorated in the Pompeiian style in memory of the king's Italian travels. The finest porcelain, bronzes, statuary, paintings, and furniture were sought out, while the gold and white library was filled with valuable books and the columned windows of the mirrored drawing room seemed to merge with the lake beyond. The cost of all this was appalling, especially in view of the king's military expenditures; a costly, unpopular, and unsuccessful war against Russia had only just ended. The Swedish treasury was depleted and the nation was exhausted. Yet Gustav III now chose to change alliances, announcing that he would lead an expedition against revolutionary France. Protest followed protest and the king, who did not like criticism, withdrew more and more to what he considered rustic simplicity.

Gustav had a large English park laid out at Haga. Its unusual design—with follies, chinoiseries, and temples as well as painted copper tents of Turkish inspiration—was the work of Fredrik Magnus Piper, who had studied landscape architecture in England at the king's expense. Here, while Desprez made sketches and the poet Carl Michael Bellman composed ballads about the idyllic life, Gustav ordered more and more costly furnishings for his pavilion and his never-to-be-completed palace. He ignored warnings of discontent among his people and lived, with a small circle of friends, a life dedicated to beauty and pleasure. Gustav III's sister in law, Hedvig Elisabet Charlotta, duchess of Södermanland, compared Haga Pavilion to a "residence for the twelve Caesars rather than for a Christian king." The fate against which his uncle Frederick the Great had long ago warned arrived and Gustav III died a victim of conspiracy. He was shot on March 16, 1792, at a masked ball at the Stockholm Opera and died thirteen days later in his Stockholm palace.

Following page:
The Mirrored Drawing Room-with its French windows, graceful columns and arches facing the lake is considered one of the most charming rooms in Sweden. The left hand pedestals with Italian urns are actually stoves, which can be stoked from the outside so as not to disturb the room's occupants. The grisaille friezes on gold background are by Louis Masreliez.

The large drawing room at Haga is decorated in Pompeiian style introduced to Sweden by Louis Masreliez. The composition—depicting Jupiter, June, Apollo, Minerva, and other gods of antiquity—are a reminder of the king's Italian travels. The chairs and sofas were also designed by Louis Masreliez and the candelabras are by I. Rung.

After the king's death, Haga Pavilion fell into decline. Over the next century, the mezzanine was destroyed, the library looted, the frescoes covered with damask, and the furnishings scattered among various other royal residences. Even the park was altered when, in the 1860s, the level of the lake fell. Tastes changed, however, and twentieth-century Sweden regretted the damage that had befallen Gustav III's masterpiece.

Today the Haga Pavilion looks much as it did in the time of Gustav III. It is not far from the Haga Palace, a medium-sized neoclassical building erected by Gustav IV Adolf, the son of Gustav III. The attractions of this palace cannot compare to those of the pavilion; they make us realize what a great loss the death of Gustav III was to Sweden's arts and artists.

The walls of the Council Chamber at Haga, decorated by Louis Masreliez, include motifs inspired by the Italian Renaissance. The table by G.A. Ditzinger as well as the sphinxes and candlesticks were among the room's original contents.

In the kings bedroom at Haga, a large painting by Alexander Roslin portrays Henry IV's meeting with the Duc de Sully, his minister. The night table by G. A. Ditzinger has a pivoting top, which could be swung across the bed to support the king's breakfast tray. The table also had extra trays to accomodate the king's visitors.

ULRIKSDAL PALACE

One of the two statues standing on the bridge in the English park.

The orangerie by Nicodemus Tessin the Younger was added in 1705 and has been slightly shortened after a fire in the nineteenth-century.

Ulriksdal Royal Palace, initially called Jakobsdal, was built in 1639 for Jakob De la Gardie by Hans Jacob Chrisler; it was sold to Queen Hedvig Eleonora in 1669. She renamed the property Ulriksdal in honor of the prince who was to have lived there and had the royal architect, Nicodemus Tessin the Elder, alter both the façade and the interior. But the prince died young and Ulriksdal, which is on the water and not far from the heart of Stockholm, became the summer home of succeeding monarchs. Oscar I and Karl XV made what they thought were improvements to the property throughout the nineteenth century, and the latter's zeal for all things Renaissance led to many unfortunate alterations of both the park and the building.

In 1864 Karl XV commissioned F. W. Scholander to build a chapel in the park, and by 1900 many irreversible changes had been made. But then Ulriksdal became the residence of a man of taste, Gustav VI Adolf, who throughout his long life worked to restore Sweden's royal dwellings. If Gustav III wished to leave his personal stamp on his dwellings, Gustav VI Adolf took pleasure in clearing away later clutter and bringing early glories back to light. Ulriksdal is only one of many examples of these efforts, but it is a particularly touching one, as the king looked upon this particular property as his home. The gardens, formal and colorful, are filled with handsome modern sculpture; the restored orangerie, the orchid house, and the severely elegant façade of the palace itself make a visit to Ulriksdal's grounds a pleasure even when the palace proper is closed to the public. Gustav VI Adolf also had a hand in the restoration of Kina and Haga, while many of his

other sensible and sensitive efforts on behalf of his nation's antiquities have yet to be chronicled. He died in 1973 but is still affectionately known in Sweden as "the old king."

Recently the "Confidence", a building in Ulriksdal's park turned into a theater in 1752 so that it might become home to Queen Lovisa Ulrika's troupe of French players, has been reactivated and to-day serves as a truly elegant setting for both plays and concerts.

Jakobsdal was originally built in 1639 for Jakob De la Gardie and was bought in 1669 by Queen Hedvig Eleonora who renamed it Ulriksdal for her grandson and commissioned Nicodemus Tessin the Elder to alter it.

ROSENDAL PALACE

The palace at Rosendal, built in 1823 for King Karl XIV Johan, stands intact today in the middle of the old royal deer park of Stockholm on Djurgården. Since 1913, it has been a museum honoring the king who built it. Even during Karl Johan's lifetime, the building was used only for dinners, military reviews, and receptions. Of its twenty rooms, only one was a bedroom.

Fredrik Blom, a military architect, used an early form of prefabrication to construct Rosendal's rooms over a four-year period. The rooms were built in sections to be assembled at the site; as they open into one another, these salons reflect a certain soldierly precision. Also evident is a nostalgia for Napoleonic France, which Karl Johan left behind in 1810 when, having been adopted by Karl XIII, he became Sweden's crown prince.

The small summer palace at Rosendal in Stockholm's Djurgården was built for King Karl XIV Johan by Fredrik Blom. The building's facade shows characteristic empire details: a colonnade, the rounded tops of the lower-story windows, and the semicircular recesses in the facade.

The garden at Rosendal was designed around this immense porphyry vase carved in the factory established by the king at Älvdalen.

Throughout the building and in the dining wing, added in 1826, arrows, armor, trophies, and eagles speak of bygone glories. There are also mementos of the Swedish king's military past—when, as Jean Baptiste Bernadotte, he had been one of Napoleon Bonaparte's more brilliant marshals. A bronze-and-procelain table in the Lantern Room, a gift from Louis Philippe in 1842, is decorated with the painting of a state chamber in the Castle of Pau in Gascony. Karl Johan who had been born in Pau, where his father was a clerk, good-naturedly had this table put in a place of honor. The Lantern Room reflects classic architectural principles. Its overall plan expresses the harmony of the square and the circle, and its large cupola, marking the center of the house, is adorned with paintings of the four seasons. In their enthusiasm, architect Blom and his patron tended to neglect such essentials as

Rosendal Palace.
The elaborated wall decorations of the
Blue Room executed by Pehr Emanuel
Limnel in 1825, are a reminder of
Karl XIV Johan's military past.

40

Considered one of the most magnificent rooms in the palace, the Red Room is decorated in a manner that combines an imperial atmosphere with elements of gothicism as seen in the grisaille frieze. The Egyptian colonnettes and mahogany furniture were copied from French models. The portrait represents King Karl XIV Johan.

Rosendal Palace.
*The kings bedroom can be seen through
the opened door of the Yellow Room, its
furnishings were originally in the Royal
Palace at Stockholm. In the foreground
is a sculpture of a baccante by E. G.
Gothe.*

corridors, walls, and pantries. Indeed, it soon became obvious that the
dining wing would require at least three additional service rooms in
order to function. In the interests of symmetry, the architect had provided none. Although it is unimpressive from without, Rosendal is a
riot of color within. There are vivid reds, blues, greens, and yellows;
flowered chandeliers; bronze, malachite, and porphyry. And almost all
of this splendor, including the huge porphyry vase on the northern
terrace, was of a local manufacture; the king owned the Älvdalen porphyry factory; only a few chandeliers and most of the clocks were imported. The damasks were also made in Sweden, Karl Johan being the
local mill's best and sometimes only customer.

Yet everything about Rosendal was supposed to be French. The
draperies were copied from pattern books published by Osmont in

The Library and Study contains Karl XIV Johan's desk mementos and collection of books.

The Sèvres table in the Lantern Room. It was a gift from France's King Louis Philippe to Karl XIV Johan in 1842. The decoration of the table top depicts the Chateau of Pau, a city that was the original home of the Bernardotte family.

Paris; the furniture was modeled on engravings by Percier and Fontaine complete with griffins and sphinxes, but the furniture has lighter, cleaner lines; there is also less bronze than is typical on French Empire furniture. The Swedish custom of leaving the center of a salon unencumbered makes for a refreshing openness. The bright, clear colors and, above all, the lightness and intimacy make Rosendal a Swedish, not a French palace—a handsome example of Karl Johan rather than Empire decoration.

TYRESÖ CASTLE

The imposing castle of Tyresö, was built around 1630 in the Renaissance style, its owner was Gabriel Oxenstierna; Tyresö was rebuilt and restored many times during the eighteenth and nineteenth centuries; it was finally restored to conform with the original concept by Isak Gustaf Clason for Marquis Lagergren.

A castle of 100 rooms, Tyresö was built between 1620 and 1633 for Gabriel Oxenstierna, the younger brother of Chancellor Axel Oxenstierna; with its four towers and enclosed courtyard, it then had an almost military character. Between 1765 and 1770, however, it was transformed for Carl Fredrik Scheffer into a rococo country seat by tearing down two of the towers and opening up the courtyard. Detached one-story wings with mansard roofs were built and the two remaining towers were lowered by one story. In 1870, one Horstadius, then the owner, had the towers gabled, and in 1892 the property was sold to Marquis Claes Lagergren, chamberlain to the Papal household. Counseled by Isak Gustaf Clason, the architect of the Nordiska Museum, Lagergren decided to restore the building's original character.

The wings were raised, the towers reconstructed, and portals added. Work was still in progress in 1930, when Lagergren died. He left the property to the Nordiska Museum, which maintains it at present.

The outcome of all this rebuilding is not entirely happy, since the new towers crowd the once detached wings and the courtyard is no longer enclosed as it was initially. Within the building as well, much is inauthentic. Why did Marquis Lagergren, who had inherited from Tyresö's other owners such works as Lambrecht Ryche's portrait of Johan III, Sergel's bust of Count Scheffer, and the Per Krafft portrait of Gustav Vasa, see fit to flesh out Tyresö's collection with so many copies? A bunch of fresh flowers stands before a copy of the portrait of Marie Antoinette painted when she was imprisoned in the Con-

Bust of Queen Marie Antoinette of France on a Gustavian console at Tyresö castle.

Corner of the Green Salon at Tyresö with Gustav III pier glass mirror and a collection of nineteenth-century royal personages and family members.

ciergerie. The late queen of France was the object of Marquis Lagergren's particular devotion and is the subject of a dozen paintings scattered throughout the castle. None of these paintings is authentic. Neither are the portraits of Axel von Fersen, Gustav III, Louis XV, Madame Pompadour, and Queen Kristina. Why should a rich man surround himself with props rather than works of art? What fantasy was acted out here?

One of the few genuine antiques to be found at Tyresö is a piece of one of Marie Antoinette's dresses. It is displayed in a ground-floor passageway in a very elaborate altarlike case that bears her initials.

Tyresö, on the Baltic Sea, is one of three properties east of Stockholm that survived the Russian raids of 1719 undamaged. It is said that the owners burned the woods around the castle and tore down one of the towers so that the invaders would think that Tyresö had already been destroyed by others.

SANDEMAR MANOR

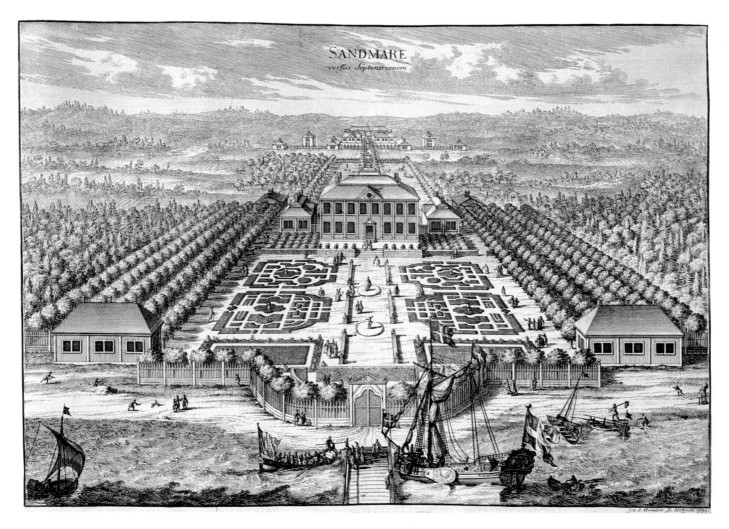

SANDMARE
versus Septentrionem

Sandemar is one of the few great manor houses that were not destroyed by the Russians in their invasion of 1719. It looks today much as it did in this engraving by Eric Dahlbergh.

Sandemar, a noble residence east of Stockholm, also escaped destruction by the invading Russians in 1719. And it is most fortunate that Sandemar did survive, for its interior is covered with seventeenth-century murals and decorations that are both rustic and refined. In the living room, gray tree in a "forest tapestry" seem to grow up the sides of white walls to the imitation stucco ceiling. The stairwell is adorned with figures of seventeenth-century peasants, in wide pants, gaiters, and broad-brimmed hats, carrying spades on their shoulders. Higher up, hunters dressed in red guard the entrance of a dining-room suite that holds a collection of royal portraits by David Klöcker Ehrenstrahl, court painter to Karl XI, Hedvig Eleonora, and Karl XII.

Ehrenstral, dubbed "the Rubens of the north," kept copies of many of the portraits and allegories he had been commissioned to paint for

the royal palaces. These smaller variations of the immense originals lend an air of grandeur to Sandemar's reception rooms. A further variation on royal themes is evident in the decoration of the Knight's Hall. The canvases here spell out the story of Solomon and are painted so as to resemble Gobelin tapestries.

Sandemar faces the Baltic, its garden—overlooking the gray, tideless sea—is still as it was when Eric Dahlberg drew it for *Svecia Antiqua et Hodierna*. There, a central statue of Neptune stands amid wooded alleyways peopled with putti. The god faces the manor house. Trident in hand, Neptune commands the Baltic, the seaway that throughout the centuries has connected Sweden to the European continent and across which the Vikings once sailed.

In the center of Sandemar's garden path to the sea Neptune stands surrounded by putti. These figures, made of white painted wood, are removed in the winter.

Sandemar Manor.
The walls of the principal drawing room are covered in painted tapestry portraying an episode from the Song of Solomon.

The Entrance Hall's grisaille ceiling imitating stucco is complemented by grisaille paintings on the wall. Two figures dressed in Swedish peasant costumes flank the entrance to the dining room. Councillor of State Gabriel von Falkenberg began building Sandemar in the late seventeenth century; much of its decoration dates from that period.

BEATELUND MANOR

The Carolinian manor house at Beatelund, surrounded by a baroque garden, was rebuilt in 1726 after the original was burned to the ground by the Russians during the invasion of 1719. Until the end of the eighteenth century, visitors to Beatelund arrived by water.

A Japanese pavilion on a hill behind the garden.

Beatelund, destroyed by the Russians in 1719, was thereafter rebuilt with taste and elegance. Partly because it is so beautifully situated, Beatelund has always inspired love in its owners. During the eighteenth century, the property belonged to the Rålamb family, one of whom, as ambassador to Turkey in 1657, became the first Swede to taste coffee. Another Rålamb who followed Karl XII to Narva and Poltava was captured and sent to Siberia, where he spent his years of imprisonment writing a French/Latin/Swedish dictionary.

On his return to Sweden, he found that his old home had been replaced by an eighteenth-century Carolinian minichateau consisting of a main building and two symmetrical wings with *säteri* roofs. Today, the ceilings of the reception rooms are decorated with painted swags and landscapes; the medallions on the salon's walls commemorate the

poets Bellman, Oxenstierna, other Swedish notables, and the library is crammed with eighteenth-century volumes.

Beatelund's buildings face the Baltic. Visitors who arrived by sea could find accomodations immediately to hand, in the detached wings. (One of these can be rented for banquets and special occasions.) Boats arriving from Stockholm are first glimpsed from the small Chinese pleasure house that stands high as a crow's nest at the back of the estate's baroque gardens.

Beatelund's gardens, whose original Carolinian design was recreated from old documents found in the Cederström archives, are a monument to Sten Westerberg, who began restoring Beatelund in 1923. Thanks to him and his family, the buildings, too, have been refurbished to approximate their original condition.

The original ceiling of the dining room at Beatelund Manor is intact, its timbered surface is painted in the Bérain style. The winter picture on the wall is by the Swedish twentieth-century painter Bruno Liljefors.

A rococo corner of the original sitting room, like that of the dining room, the ceiling is painted in the Bérain style.

GRIPSHOLM CASTLE

The present Gripsholm Castle stands on an island in Lake Mälaren across from the town of Mariefred. It has had several predecessors. The first castle, built by Bo Jonsson (Grip) in 1377, burned in 1434. Some decades before this disaster, in 1396, Queen Margareta I had issued an edict forbidding the nobility to erect new towers or fortresses. Although the great lords often ignored this law, Gripsholm Castle was still a ruin when Gustav Eriksson Vasa, a nobleman escaping from the Danes, asked the Carthusian monks of the nearby monastery for shelter. But the monks refused to take him in. Gustav did not forget this slight and—in 1523, when he had become the first of the Vasa kings—he rescinded the monks' charter. In 1537, he began building a royal fortress on the propitious site of the old castle, close to Stockholm and dominating both Lake Mälaren and the approach to the Baltic.

An irregular hexagon built of brick around a courtyard, Gripsholm Castle incorporates four asymmetrical towers and to this day boasts a drawbridge, gun slots, and ornate Renaissance cannons. Gripsholm, like all Vasa castles, exudes a feeling of power. Even today it is best approached by water. In the summer, an antique steamer called the *Mariefred* sails daily from Stockholm's city hall to the town opposite the castle. The castle itself looms up over lake and town, its great "Grip" tower threatening all invaders. Enlarged and enhanced in later centuries, Gripsholm retains the spirit of its prime builder and is most impressive on a rainy day, when it appears as a huge, rosy abstraction between the slate-gray water and steel-gray sky.

Gustav Vasa cared nothing for decorations, being content to live in a wooden hut while the three-meter-thick walls of his fortress rose around him. The same could not be said of his sons. As handsome as he was ostentatious, Erik XIV thought of himself as a humanist. He was an accomplished poet and at the time of his father's death (1560) had just left for England to seek the hand of Queen Elizabeth I. Unfortunately Erik soon quarreled with his half brothers, the future Johan III and Karl IX, and had Johan confined in the prison tower of Gripsholm. Here, in a luxurious suite of rooms, Johan's son Sigismund III of Sweden and Poland was born in 1566; here in 1571, Erik was, in turn, imprisoned by Johan.

Johan, known as "the builder king," concentrated on his many other castles, which included Stockholm, Vadstena, Kalmar, and Uppsala; it

Among the many costume portraits at Gripsholm Castle, this one is of Ulla von Höpken as she appeared in Gustav III's play, "Tha Valour of Gustav Adolf" which was first performed in January 1783. Ulla von Höpken was the sister of Count Axel von Fersen, the favorite of Marie Antoinette.

Gripsholm Castle.

The Neo-classic theatre hung in one of the largest towers at Gripsholm was executed by Eric Palmstedt, one of Sweden's great eighteenth-century architects. The stage is flanked by J. T. Sergel's sculptures representing Thalia, the muse of comedy and Melpomene, muse of tragedy. The set on stage was designed by L. J. Desprez for the original production of Gustav III's play "Queen Kristina".

One of the hatches or "lorgnettes" that were constructed to allow the king's servants to see his plays from hidden seats inserted within the ceiling of the theater.

Gripsholm Castle.
Detail of Duke Karl's Chamber.

was the youngest brother, Duke Karl of Södermanland (later Karl IX), who restored and refurbished Gripsholm after he had moved the captive Erik XIV elsewhere. Duke Karl's bedroom is still intact, as are its few furnishings. The restoration of the Hall of State and the other rooms in the Vasa apartments was carried to excess during the last century. However, these rooms are furnished with authentic Renaissance pieces, many of them taken from other Vasa castles.

In the seventeenth century, castles began to decline in importance and Gripsholm became a dower house. Karl IX's widow, Queen Katerina, lived here, as did the widowed Queen Hedvig Eleonora. She loved architecture, as we have seen at Drottningholm and Ulriksdal, and took delight in making alterations—adding wings or extra stories—even though she seldom spent more than a month a year at the castle throughout her long (1660-1715) widowhood.

On Hedvig Eleonora's death, Gripsholm reverted to the crown. Crown Princess Lovisa Ulrika received Gripsholm as part of her dowry, but she had no real interest in the property and ultimately exchanged it for another estate. During the years of her ownership, more and more paintings from the royal collections were stored at Gripsholm, and by 1775 over three hundred portraits had joined those of the Vasa kings in the castle's galleries. Among the most amusing is the "hen" portrait, deaccessioned from Drottningholm because the artist, Johan Pasch, had painted the crown princess's ladies-in-waiting as chickens.

From 1773 to 1785, Gustav III spent much of his time at Gripsholm. He expanded the picture collection to include portraits of

prominent Swedes. Those of Carolus Linnaeus, Emmanuel Swedenborg, the poet Bellman, and Johan Tobias Sergel, the court sculptor, were added to the ever-growing collection that remains at the castle today. Gustav III also pressed his architects to render Gripsholm "worthy of a court." Reception rooms were refurbished and the king's study established in the Vasa tower. Jean Eric Rehn redecorated the White Hall and enlarged the queen's wing, the most beautiful rooms of which were furnished for Queen Sofia Magdalena, Gustav III's Danish consort. The Gustavian rooms in Gripsholm are among the loveliest of their kind in Sweden, their bright colors and graceful gilded furniture contrasting with the dark, heavy furnishings of the Vasa apartments and the warlike character of the castle itself. Unfortunately the wing that housed Gustav III's cavaliers—a series of bedrooms complete with their original furniture, stoves, painted canvas walls, and nettle-flax curtains—is not currently open to the public.

No matter what his dwelling, Gustav III, "the player king," had to have a theater, so first Adelcrantz and then Erik Palmstedt were given the difficult task of hanging a round playhouse within one of Gustav Vasa's thick-walled towers. In suspending this theater above the newly decorated White Hall, the architects faced the risk that the tower might collapse or the floor buckle. Palmstedt found the solution: he expanded the stage into the queen's wing and chose light building materials, relying on trompe l'oeil, half columns, and mirrors for the decoration of this theater which remains in use to the present day. Thus, eighteen years after the opening of the blue, white, and gold court theater at Drottningholm, Gustav III had a red, white, and gold theater of his own. Of necessity, the audiences were small. Above four semicircular rows of benches, two tiers of boxes accomodated those courtiers who were lucky enough to be invited. The applause of the "happy few" was echoed by that of the royal servants, who were seated in a gallery concealed within the playhouse ceiling; through octagonal lunettes, they were able to see the king perform (according to Axel von Fersen the Younger) as Rhadamite, Cinna, the high priest of Jerusalem. Johan Tobias Sergel's large statues of Thalia and Melpomene, which flank the stage at Gripsholm, witnessed the premieres of Gustav III's many plays. *The Valor of Gustav Adolf* was first performed by courtiers here on January 11, 1783. A series of small paintings in the theater's vestibule commemorate the appearance of Gustav's courtiers as actors in this and other plays.

After Gustav III's tragic death, there were no more royal theatricals at Gripsholm for a long time. His unfortunate son Gustav IV Adolf was imprisoned in the fortress after the bloodless revolution of 1809. With the accession of the Bernadotte family, the castle became more a museum than a residence. Karl XIV Johan transformed the ever-growing conglomeration of portraits into an official "Swedish Pantheon." Today the collection housed in the castle and at the nearby high school includes portraits not only of Swedish kings, courtiers, and foreign potentates but also of notable who have enriched the country's life. Emmanuel Swedenborg and Adolf Badin (Queen Lovisa Ulrika's West Indian page) have been joined by Jenny Lind, Dag Hammarskjöld, Jussi Björling, Gunnar and Alva Myrdal, and numerous other distinguished Swedes. At present there are about 3,500 portraits in the collection.

Under the direction of F. Lilljekvist, Gripsholm was restored at the end of the nineteenth century. His "reconstructions" included Dutch dormers above enlarged windows and the redecoration of the Vasa apartments in late-nineteenth-century style. Since 1950, various curators have been correcting Lilliekvist's additions in the interests of authenticity. Since Gripsholm is a royal residence of capital historic importance, it is likely that further generations will be eager to correct the correctors.

Every visit to Gripsholm reveals some new aspect of the castle. In the last decade, the armories have been completely reordered in a manner that would have pleased the castle's founder. And each new year brings more portraits of honored Swedish citizens to augment the riches of this shrine, commemorating those who have best served their nation.

Gripsholm Castle.

The King's Bedroom was originally created for Duchess Kristina the Elder. The coffer ceiling and wall decorations are of this period. The room adorned on the left hand-side by a Torgaw tapestry bearing a royal coat of arms, hangs above a remarkable Japanese lacquered chest, gift from the Dutch government to Gustav II Adolf.
A seventeenth-century standing clock is located in front of the tapestry at the end of the room.

STUREHOV MANOR

Sturehov Manor was purchased in 1778 by Johan Liljecrantz, Gustav III's finance minister. He immediately commissioned Carl Fredrik Adelcrantz to build him a suitable house between the then existing wings of the manor, and Adelcrantz excelled himself in this project, remodeling the wings to form a beautifully proportioned whole. Sturehov remains to this day a near-perfect example of late-eighteenth-century domestic architecture.

Liljecrantz was not only a man of taste but also the coproprietor of the Marieberg factory, which manufactured glazed ceramic stoves as well as table china between 1758 and 1788. Not surprisingly, the stoves at Sturehov were made at this factory. Today, about thirty original Marieberg stoves remain in Sweden, seventeen of them at Sturehov, many in the rooms for which they were designed. These stoves, made

The Octagonal Dining Room was designed by J. E. Rehn. This room is particularly noteworthy for its columned stove made in a style which became fashionable in the 1780s. Most of the chairs were designed by the cabinet maker Erik Öhrmark in 1777.

The Red Cabinet at the far end of the enfilade of rooms on the first floor has a charming view over the garden and lake Mälaren. The rose pattern on the stove is a typical design of its day.

of white ceramic tiles decorated with floral or architectural motifs, are so much esteemed that the one in the Yellow Salon has been reproduced on a Swedish postage stamp. They are also interesting in that several still stand on the wooden feet that were rightly banned by the government as fire hazards at the end of the eighteenth century.

But there is more to this lovely property than stoves. Liljecrantz, who in 1770 prepared and carried through Gustav III's financial reforms, enjoyed his monarch's confidence and was often his host. Sturehov can be reached by road and water from Stockholm, Gripsholm, and Tullgarn. The king must have found it a welcome stopping place on his travels. One can even see the whole house as a subtle compliment to Gustav III. Although the king's portrait is nowhere in evidence, Johan Tobias Sergel's monumental busts of

Gustav's favorite ancestors, Gustav Vasa and Gustav II Adolf, dominate the Octagonal Salon. This room retains its original stove, furnishings, and marquetry floor to the present day. Because Sturehov is today the property of the city of Stockholm, the other half-dozen reception rooms have been filled with period antiques lent by various museums. The main manor house is used today for small official conferences and receptions, while larger groups can be accommodated in the separate kitchen wing, which, with C. F. Adelcrantz's façade, retains its seventeenth-century character and Carolinian painted ceiling. The kitchen wing functioned as such until 1918. Now it serves as a dining room and can be rented for private parties. There can surely be no nicer place for a summer fête than Sturehov park. Behind the main house, green lawns run down to the water between rows of pear and apple trees. Here Liljecrantz would have waited for his royal guest, and here Gustav would have indulged in the sweets and sherbets he loved while discussing the nation's business. For he was well served by his minister, who—unlike Louis XIV's Fermier-General Nicholas Fouquet—kept his dwelling place modest.

Beautiful, but modest. At first glance Sturehov looks much like any other country house. Then it becomes clear that although the wings are built in wood, the foundation of the main house is made of pink sand stone and that a kind of perfection has been achieved here that the builder of Vaux-le-Vicomte could never have imagined.

Sturehov Manor.

An elegant bedroom used by the lady of the house later became a drawing room. The decorative wall paintings are by L. Bolander. The sofa and chairs are from the eighteenth century.

HÖRNINGSHOLM CASTLE

The castle on the cliff dominates the island of Mörkö.

Erected on the ruins of a medieval castle, the eighteenth-century manor house at Hörningsholm stands on a promontory above a deepwater passage to the Baltic Sea. The medieval structure was transformed into a German Renaissance castle, one of the largest private dwellings in Sweden, with a remarkable garden. The castle was destroyed during the Russian invasion of 1719.

In the 1740s Nils Bonde, Hörningsholm's owner, commissioned Sweden's great rococo architect Carl Hårleman to build a more modern house on the ruins of the old castle. Hårleman created a manor house of classic symmetry, allowing the natural beauty of the setting to dominate the property.

The fourteenth-century cellar and the sixteenth-century bastion overhanging the cliff remain to remind us of Hörningsholm's past.

TULLGARN PALACE

Seen from the seaside, with its double staircase leading to its grand courtyard, Tullgarn Palace was designed by the French born architect Joseph Gabriel Destain in 1719 for the De la Gardie family. The Palace was rebuilt and refurnished in neo-classical style for Duke Fredrik Adolf, brother of Gustav III.

Tullgarn Palace.
The Blue Cabinet. The Italian landscape engravings in this Gustavian room are glued directly to the walls, these were mementos of Duke Fredrik Adolf's journey to Italy. The panels of nymphs and fauns are copied from a book entitled "Le Pitture Antiche d'Ercolaneo."

The Red Drawing Room. Still a perfect eighteenth-century court set adorned by a uniquely beautiful parquet floor and a large three fold silk screen created by Queen Lovisa Ulrika.

The palace proper stands at the very end of an isthmus in the Trosa Archipelago, its main front facing the sea. First owned by the Sture family and then completely rebuilt in 1719 for Councillor Magnus Julius De la Gardie, the new building was designed by Joseph Gabriel Destain, a French fortification officer who also designed two other palaces in the Swedish province of Södermanland.

The wings were completely rebuilt during the late eighteenth century, even the roof of the main building was transformed, so that now the palace is a harmonious whole as it faces the Baltic. In 1772 Tullgarn was purchased by the government and placed at the disposal of Gustav III's youngest brother, Duke Fredrik Adolf. It has remained a royal summer residence ever since and is still used by King Karl XVI Gustaf.

Tullgarn's courtyard stands open to the sea, but most modern visitors reach the palace from the land, first driving, then walking, through the forty-four landscaped acres that adjoin the castle. The park is also the site of an excellent inn and an orangerie built in the 1840s. On the lawn in front of the palace entrance, flower plantings form a royal crown over the blue and gold coat of arms of Gustav V (1858-1950) and the yellow and maroon escutcheon of his queen, Viktoria of Baden. This monarch, who chose Tullgarn as his summer residence in 1881 while still crown prince, along with his queen, redecorated parts of the palace in nineteenth-century style.

In the 1880s the ground-floor vestibule was altered to house a very handsome collection of seventeenth and eighteenth century Dutch tiles. A stone mosaic copy of Pompeiis's first-century *Cave Canem* was set in the floor of the entry. It is recorded that this mosaic was made of pebbles picked up by Queen Viktoria and her ladies in waiting during trips to Italy.

The lower story contains Gustav V's smoking and writing rooms and, to the left of the entry, Queen Viktoria's breakfast room, created around 1890 in the style of a south German beer cellar; this room remains intact to this day. The monarchs and their friends painted coats of arms and garlands of flowers on the paneling and on the walls. The heavily carved furniture is German and the dark-green tile stove Dutch. The spirit of 1890 that rules supreme in the breakfast room has been muted and controlled in the upper story. Here we see the hand of Queen Viktoria's eldest son, Gustav VI Adolf. An archeologist by avocation, he did all he could to restore the Gustavian elegance of Tullgarn. The main staircase is a good example of the sureness of this monarch's taste. Gustav V and Queen Viktoria had covered Anders Hultgren's eighteenth-century murals of Greek gods with peasant fabrics given to them as a wedding present. Their son, however, freed Venus, Apollo, and Diana from their drapery, and today they look down in greeting upon arriving guests. The main dining room on the second floor is decorated in muted tones with a blue and white frieze, taken from Wedgewood pottery, that gracefully accents the simplicity of the huge room—uncluttered and full of light—making it a perfect setting for neoclassic banquets.

In the billiard room next door, nineteenth-century extravance has been tamed by more modern taste. The paneling and ceiling frieze date from the eighteenth century. Queen Desirée's French lemonwood cottage piano (Mercier, Paris, 1834) has been adorned with medallion portraits of her and her husband, King Karl XIV Johan, and with India ink drawings depicting the sheet music of her various compositions.

A painting signed by Krepensky in 1909 depicts Tsar Nicolas II's visit to Tullgarn in June of that year. The Blue Drawing Room was redecorated about 1890 in the then fashionable German neorococo style, but the small anteroom and the large Red Drawing Room have retained their eighteenth-century character. The latter is graced by a green and white frieze of wedgewoodlike dancers and a very beautiful parquet floor—made of alder, juniper, and birch—with a central medallion of three antique damsels, one of whom is carrying a basket of cupids. The furniture is all of the same period, as are the paintings. A large threefold silk screen in one corner illustrates Queen Lovisa Ulrika's skill as a needlewoman.

Tullgarn's State Bedroom was planned and designed by the Masreliez brothers. The walls are covered with boiserie and the gilded bed is placed in an alcove crowned by a dove, indicating that this room was occupied by a lady. The Blue Cabinet, a lovely small room beside the State Bedroom, is decorated with a series of colored engravings, mostly of Roman buildings as they appeared in the 1770s. The floor of this room is covered with a canvas painted blue and white and decorated with pictures of various gods amid foliage. This is the work of Anders Hultgren, as are the handsome window embrasures, doors, and paneling, all alive with birds and flowers. Next door we find a

Tullgarn Palace.
The Green Bedroom is particularly noteworthy for its gilded boisseries and the green striped bed made in 1790 by J. L. Masreliez.

A corner of the duke's study. On the right the portrait of a Prussian princess stands above a drop front marquetry desk by Georg Haup. To the left of the duke's sister-in-law Queen Hedwig Elisabeth Charlotta is pictured above a lacquered writing table and etagère by Nils Dahlin.

small bedroom all in white and gold, with bright-green silk that was designed for Gustav III's youngest brother, Duke Fredrik Adolf. The carved bed bears the arms of the province of Östergötland and the alcove is crowned by a triomphe centered around a helmet.

Throughout Tullgarn's second story, Gustav VI Adolf's respect for the past and attention to detail are much in evidence. Thanks to him, it may be said that Tullgarn today is as much a monument to Swedish elegance as it is a comfortable summer home for the nation's monarch. Not lacking in humor, he left one of his mother's more extraordinary purchases exactly as it was. Touring the castle, we happen upon a carved wooden chandelier in the shape of a mermaid surrounded by elkhorns.

THUREHOLM MANOR

Thureholm, once an island, tops a ramp over a now empty moat. it was built in 1728 by Carl Hårleman for the Bielke family.

A large, beautiful, well-proportioned house with six detached wings, Thureholm was built in 1728 by Carl Hårleman for the Bielke family. Hårleman had just returned from his first trip to France and was probably expected to produce a French chateau; instead, he followed the Carolinian spirit of the preexisting building (which had been burnt by the Russians in 1719) to the point of incorporating some of the old walls in the new castle. Three stories tall, with a *säteri* roof echoed in its wings, Thureholm tops a large cobblestone courtyard that is reached by a ramp inclined over what long ago was a moat.

The manor's Great Salon has elegant rococo panels encompassing portraits of Swedish kings. Other rooms are adorned with chinoiserie landscapes painted in the 1730s.

The beautiful rococo kitchen is painted with blue and white clouds and flowering shrubs growing up the wall.

Antique scale in the kitchen.

Thureholm's red, green, blue, and gold tapestries woven around 1700 at Beauvais to Jean Berain's design now grace the Oval Salon of Stockholm's Statehouse and its large collection of Chinese porcelain and Swedish faïence (from the Rörstrand and Marieberg works) have been dispersed. The manor's charming rustic rococo kitchen is decorated with painted shrubs, trees, and floral motifs.

ELGHAMMAR MANOR

Elghammar manor seen from the garden side, was built from plans made by Giacomo Quarenghi for Field Marshall Count Christoffer von Stedingk, Swedish ambassador at the court of St. Petersburg. What was initially the manor house became a wing of the much expanded house. While the interior of the original wing remained traditionally Swedish in its decoration and furnishings, the major new addition to the house was made in the neo-classic style.

The waterside pavilion on Lake Lockvattnet.

Carved in large letters on the peristyle above Elghammar's main entrance are the words *More Parentum* (in the manner of our forefathers). This was the family motto of Curt Bogislaus Ludvig Christoffer von Stedingk (1746-1837), who, in 1794, had the present manor built to plans drawn up by Giacomo Quarenghi, the Italian architect responsible for the construction in Russia of both St. Petersburg's Alexander Palace and Tsarskoiselo. Architecturally, this Latin phrase seems inappropriate, as Elghammar, far from being built in a traditional way, is actually the major Palladian country house in Sweden. A unique and successful adaptation of a foreign style, the building reflects not so much the personality as the point of view of its builder.

Elghammar Manor.

The Great Galley dominates the central portion of the house. The large portrait shows Gustav III in his coronation robes while the smaller portrait is of Joseph Fouché, Napoleon's Minister of Police. The Gallery's four white ceramic stoves are crowned with statues designed by J.T. Sergel.

For von Stedingk was a truly international Swede. Born a baron, he began his adult life as a soldier. Like Axel von Fersen the Younger, he served with Lafayette in America (1778). Having distinguished himself on field of battle, he was wounded and invalided out to the Swedish legation in France. He was an excellent linguist and at one time was taken up by Marie Antoinette when she was attempting to distract the attention of French court gossips from her romance with Fersen. No one was deceived by the queen's maneuver, and although "little Stedingk" hoped for a moment to replace "tall Axel" (the descriptions are Gustav III's) as favorite, he soon resigned himself to the role of friend. We find him petitioning via Madame de Boufflers in 1781 for a Swedish royal pension to defray his expenses in France. Gustav III answered that "a man of rank is always better off at home than in foreign parts" and ordered von Stedingk back to Sweden, where he enjoyed a brilliant career both as a soldier and a diplomat. He was a front-line commander against the Russians in the 1788-1790 war and, after the declaration of peace, was sent as ambassador to St. Petersburg. There, his personal success with the *"Semiramis* of the North" was so great that he ended by serving in the Russian capital from 1790 to 1808 and from 1809 to 1811. During these twenty-one years, von Stedingk collected many beautiful pieces of Russian furniture to enrich the collections of Elghammar. Indeed, the left-hand wing is known as the Russian wing. His discerning eye singled out to the beautiful chandelier (made by I. A. S. Fischer in St. Petersburg in 1793) that hangs in the Blue Salon. Catherine II of Russia became a personal friend; she used to give von Stedingk copies of the Russian

A presentation portrait of Gustav IV in the Great Gallery. An empire gilded harp stands in the corner.

books published during her reign (1762-1796). This large group of rare volumes enriches the collection of eighteenth-century incunabula lodged in the gold and white library which viewed from within, seems to hang over the lake. This magical effect of floating on water was achieved by Elghammar's present owner, the Duke d'Otrante, by cutting back the thick growth of trees that once separated the mansion from the surrounding lake. The name d'Otrante reminds us that Elghammar passed by marriage in 1875 to the descendants of Joseph Fouché, another fascinating figure of the eighteenth century.

Fouché (1759-1820) was born in Brittany and educated by the Oratorian brothers. He became a revolutionary and in 1793 was a member of the French National Assembly that condemned Louis XVI to death. Riding on the wave of the Revolution, Fouché became minister of police under first the Consulate and then the Empire. He was named a duke by Napoleon, and Louis XVIII confirmed his title, which Fouché's son kept when he came to Sweden at the invitation of King Karl XIV Johan. Ultimately, Athanase, duke d'Otrante, became chamberlain to King Oscar I, and it is from him that the present duke is descended. There are many souvenirs of Fouché at Elghammar: his bed; a portrait signed by Claude Dubuge, showing him with the Legion of Honor; swords, pistols, even a rapier with a gold and lapis lazuli buckle signed by Nicholas Noel Boulet.

Another painting of Fouché, in Napoleonic court dress, stands in the great gallery opposite Lorens Pasch's large duplicate portrait of Gustav III in his coronation robes. Studying the latter, we cannot but see whose spirit dominates Elghammar. It is a pity that the Swedish

Elghammar Manor.
The great Russian double bed imported by Ambassador von Stedingk is canopied and draped in white, gold and pink silks.

king did not live to see the environment that von Stedingk created for himself. Gustav would have approved Elghammar's monumental stables and the care with which the preexisting manor house was incorporated into the right-hand wing. He would have been enchanted by the overall elegance and openess of the estate as harmonious whole.

Gustav III, who was thinking in classical terms at the time of his death, would have seconded all his companion's choices. The king had several rare capacities: first, the farsightedness to allow his men of talent their freedom in the great world of "abroad"; second, the charm to coax them into returning to their homeland; and third, the wit to employ them in a manner that enhanced their experience and enriched their country. Curt Bogislaus Ludvig Christoffer von Stedingk was made a count in 1809 and a court chamberlain in 1811.

ÅKERÖ MANOR

Carl Gustav Tessin bought Åkerö in 1747. The plans for the main house were drawn by Carl Hårleman while the wings were designed by Tessin. The building's peach and rose eighteenth-century colors have been newly restored.

The long linden tree alley leads through golden wheat fields to the main house.

A view of the lake Yungaren from the garden.

When, in 1747, Count Carl Gustav Tessin (1695-1770) bought Åkerö island from the Sparre family, his wife, Ulla Sparre, had good reason to quote him as calling the large stone manor house they found on the property "a huge bats' nest." Tessin, the son and grandson of famous architects and an architect himself, tore down the building and commissioned Carl Hårleman to erect a rococo villa on the site. Work began in 1750 on so grand a scale that Tessin was forced to sell his art collection to finance the completion of what was to be his *ile des delices*. The phrase is French, as were Carl Gustav's artistic sympathies. Although he might refer to other members of the royal inner circle as "our Frenchmen," he himself had been greatly influenced by the years he spent as Swedish ambassador to the court of Louis XV. The books, paintings, drawings, coins, and objets d'art he purchased during those years are today an important part of the Swedish national collections.

What remained to furnish Tessin's country seat sufficed to create considerable opulence; it was compared, by Daniel Tilast, to the queen's collection at Drottningholm. Tessin continued improving the property, which became his residence. His love of the extraordinary became so costly that he was eventually forced to sell Åkerö to Axel Sparre, his brother in law, who allowed him to continue in residence there until his death in 1770. Åkerö manor's paintings by Nattier, Largillière, and Rosselin have been sold, as has the Gianbologna statue that once graced the entrance hall. But the setting created for them still offers testimony to the introduction of French *agrément* into Swedish country life. Åkerö manor is today a portrait of the man who built

Åkerö Manor.
A detail of the house—the juxstaposition
of a window and a niche is considered
a signature of Hårleman's architectural
style.

it. Unlike Skokloster or Tidö, it is not a public place but stands ready
to welcome the "happy few" rather than a stream of petitioners. There
is a certain eccentricity in the building, as Hårleman had wanted to
build single-story wings on either side of the main edifice; but Tessin
imposed second stories and lived to regret them. We know a lot about
the building of Åkerö from Tessin's diaries and correspondence and
from the drawings that he and Hårleman passed back and forth to
each other for comments.

Carl Gustaf Tessin had always thought of Åkerö as a haven from the
cares of court life. When, in the course of the 1750s, he fell into un-
warranted disfavor with King Adolf Fredrik and above all Queen
Lovisa Ulrika, he found himself spending more and more time at his
country retreat. A man with many friends and many interests, he kept
in touch with the world by turning Åkerö into a welcome stopping
place for his fellow courtiers on their way to or from southern Europe.
"The old count," as he became known, was held in great esteem by all,
and not least by the future Gustav III, whose first tutor he had been.
On the eve of Tessin's death, we find the crown prince petitioning
Count Axel von Fersen the Elder, then head of government, to restore

Tessin's ambassadorial pension. Gustav III loved and revered the man by whom he had been instructed from the age of five, in both French and Swedish, on virtue and leadership. For whether Tessin wrote to the young prince in the form of fables or addressed him on the competence of painters and scientists, he always spoke to the child as one who would become "the friend, the delight, the ornament, the blessing, the hope, and the protector of your subjects." Even at age six, Gustav was not too young to be reminded of the excellence of "my worthy friend Doctor Linnaeus" and the joys of collecting natural specimens. At Åkerö, a large room on the main floor sheltered Tessin's collection of shells and minerals. One of Tessin's charming letters to the young prince is about classification and the uses of the nautilus (first drawn and then named in Latin, French, Italian, and Swedish). As an example, the writer points out to the young Prince that even "as a Swede is a Swede, whether he dwells in a magnificent palace or a miserable cottage, so a snail is and will be a snail . . . whatever [its] shell may be . . . ."

The home that Carl Gustav Tessin built for himself was both French and Swedish. The impressive formal entrance hall is adorned by

Åkerö Manor.
An original corner cupboard in the main living room painted by Olof Fridsberg. This amusing tromp l'oeil technique covers the entire cupboard: on top, a cupid playing chimney sweep is coming through a round window, above a lacquered cabinet below which two figures of Chinese mandarins have been painted in the style of Boucher.

Hierpe's wrough-iron staircase. The main salon's Pompeiian decorations were taken, by Olof Friedsberg, from designs by L. J. Lorrain. Elaborate Swedish marble floors enrich the main reception suites. Over the mantle of the main salon's fireplace is a wall painting of Diogenes and Alexander, illustrating the philosopher's indifference to royal offers of patronage—and undoubtedely Tessin's disappointment with royal ingratitude. Another salon is decorated with rococo chinoiseries inspired by Boucher. The countess's dwelling quarters were transformed around 1900. Happily a corner of her cabinet, now in the living room, remains to illustrate Carl Gustav's inquisitive intelligence and interest in trompe l'oeil. Here a painted cupid disguised as a chimney sweep hovers above a lacquer chest and two painted Chinese gentlemen that Tessin found "more impressive" than similar but smaller efforts by Berain and Watteau. Tessin derived great satisfaction from furnishing Åkerö. When he found he could not maintain Läckö castle, he ensconced the trompe l'oeil panels he had ordered from Johan Pasch in Åkerö's north wing, where he also installed his library and a winter bedroom with a tile floor. These paintings of flutes, books, clothing, and clocks are perhaps the finest examples of trompe l'oeil in Sweden. They also offer a good indication of the degree of luxury that Tessin, despite his troubles, was able to enjoy throughout his life.

Detail of tromp l'oeil neo-classical wall paintings by Olof Fridsberg after L. J. Lorrain which occupy the four walls of the manor's main salon.

Åkerö Manor.
In one of the wings Tessin placed Johan Pasch's tromp l'oeil murals on canvas that were originally intended for the castle at Läckö. The stove comes from Nyköping factory.

On the right a musical monkey, one of the details that illustrate the high quality of Johan Pasch's murals.

Åkerö's beauty is best appreciated on a summer day like that of June 3, 1769, when the king, queen, and Tessin's beloved crown prince came to call on him in his "country retreat." A marble plaque in the upstairs hall commemorates this visit, which must have been more sad than happy. Carl Gustav Tessin had been one of the groomsmen who, in 1744, had escorted Adolf Fredrik's bride from Berlin. He had risen high in her esteem, only to be repudiated, and now, at his life's end, could reach Lovisa Ulrika only through her son. Much of the best in Gustav III had been encouraged by his tutor. Generosity, magnanimity, courage, and forgiveness were, with love of knowledge, the key virtues the tutor had urged upon the small child. These qualities certainly distinguished Carl Gustav Tessin's various careers as ambassador, chancellor, architect, and builder. His diaries, correspondence, and collections show us a most extraordinarily agreeable man.

At the end of its magnificent linden avenue, Åkerö manor glows cream and peach among its wheat fields. The buildings newly restored to their eighteenth-century colors greet us today as they did their master over two hundred years ago.

ERICSBERG CASTLE

Ericsberg castle is ascribed to Nicodemus Tessin the Elder although no documented proof exists to confirm his hand. The building was extended in the 1670s on an existing three story structure.

This richly furnished entailed castle stands in the center of the largest privately owned agricultural complex in Sweden. An ultramodern timber mill stands near the entrance to the property, rendering Ericsberg's 20,000 hectares of woodland profitable.

After a long drive, through well-kept farmlands, the castle comes into view across a lake. The visitor must drive around the lake past a particularly lovely antique mill and up a linden alleyway to reach the castle proper. Viewed from the lake side, Ericsberg is a huge four-story building with four wings and a double staircase; on the garden

The famous original octagonal bathroom in Ericsberg castle is a magnificent representation of the Baroque period in Sweden. In the center of the room is a marble basin covered by a cupola with rich stucco work. The surrounding walls alternate between statues of putti tucked in niches and stucco pilasters.

side, the 1660 Dutch baroque façade is in perfect harmony with the formal grounds and Fredrik Wilhelm Scholander's classical fountain. Nicodemus Tessin the Elder is reputed to have been the building's architect. Carlo Carove, the seventeenth-century Italian stuccoist, worked throughout Ericsberg's interior. His masterpiece is the castle's octagonal bathroom, complete with copper tubs, pilasters, and a statue of Venus. The castle houses historical riches unequaled in Sweden, including several extraordinary libraries.

BIBY MANOR

One of the oldest wooden manor houses in Sweden seen from its garden.

The eighteenth century family tree of the Turkish Sultans in the Turkish salon.

Erected in the early seventeenth century, Biby is probably the oldest wooden manor house in all of Sweden. Painted the same red as many Swedish houses, it has been altered and added to at various times and is surrounded by several timbered farm buildings that stand on independent foundations. The main building originally consisted of two houses with a gate between them. At the end of the seventeenth century, these two houses were connected. When, in 1782, Biby passed to the Celsing family, Gustav Celsing made them the center of the property. Beneath a nineteenth-century *säteri* roof adorned by three tall chimneys, the second story projects over the one below. Behind its rustic exterior, Biby is a treasure trove of historic riches. The space originally occupied by the connecting gate is now home to a Turkish salon complete with sofas and landscape paintings of Turkey in the eighteenth century. Here, the surroundings of Constantinople and the famous gardens along the Bosporus, can be seen as they appeared to the three members of the Celsing family who served as Swedish ambassadors to the Grande Porte. One hundred and two paintings of Turkish subjects are scattered throughout the house. One of the most interesting illustrates the reception of Gustav Celsing (wearing Turkish robes, a white periwig, and a tricorn hat) by the ruling Sultan Ahmed III. A family tree of the sultans is of particular interest, as is the portrait of Mustapha Agha, the Turkish ambassador to Sweden, painted by Georg Engelhardt Schroder in 1727. One of Biby's two libraries houses a rare watercolor likeness of Count Alexander Bonneval (1675-1747), the French soldier of fortune who ended his life in

Constantinople as Ahmed Pasha, commander of the sultan's artillery. A gold and silver embroidered caftan, presented to Gustav Celsing by the sultan as a souvenir of his reception as ambassador, stands out among Biby's collection of Turkish objects. The manor house is much more than a receptacle of Turkish exotica; among its Swedish memorabilia are Karl XI's leather games case and many royal Swedish portraits, rich furniture, and painted ceilings, all hidden behind simple well-weathered, red-painted wood walls.

"The gardens by the Bosphorous," one of the over one-hundred paintings imported by the Celsing family to Biby Manor.

STORA SUNDBY CASTLE

View of the castle complete with four large towers and twelve small towers as ordered by Charles de Geer.

In 1830 Carl de Geer of Leufsta wanted to please his wife Countess Ulrika Sprengtporten, who, like many other ladies of that era, was enamored of the works of the then universally admired British author Sir Walter Scott. Therefore de Geer asked J. F. Robinson, an English architect, to transform the abandoned sixteenth century castle at Stora Sundby into a romantic setting worthy of the lady's dreams. Robertson proceeded to design what he explained was an early Norman facade, creating a castle grander than anything in *Ivanhoe* or *The Talisman*.

Stora Sundby has four large towers, twelve small towers, fifty-two rooms, and three hundred and sixty-five windows. The towers' copper roofs are crowned with copper crosses and the huge Hall of Chivalry, which had been first created in 1675 for Axel Sparre, was refurbished in the spirit of *The Bride of Lammermoor*. Nine hunting scenes in the manner of Frans Snyders adorn the walls, wooden chandeliers carved in the form of elk and stag heads, completed by real antlers, hang from painted green iron arms above a checkerboard floor, as if anticipating the reenactment of the third act of *Lucia*.

Unfortunately Robinson never left England to supervise the building, nor did he take any interest in the furnishing of the interior of

the castle. This task was left to Abraham Nyström, Stora Sundby's local builder. Nyström admired the rococo and Gustavian styles of the preceding century, and the gilded salons he produced never made Mrs. de Geer happy. The rooms were rich and even opulent, but they were not romantic or Gothic. In no way did they match Stora Sundby's exterior.

The Hall of Chivalry at Stora Sundby was first created in 1675, revised in the 1830s.

STRÖMSHOLM PALACE

Engraving from
Svecia Antiqua et Hodierna. The palace
was built in 1660 by Queen Hedvig
Eleonora on property she had received
as a wedding gift from her husband
King Karl X Gustav. A century later,
Princess Sofia Magdalena of Danmark
received Strömsholm Palace on the
occasion of her marriage to the future
Gustav III.

Details from panels in the Strömsholm
Chinese Salon.

Strömsholm Palace, which has been royal property since the days of Gustav Vasa, is situated on an artificial island in the Kolbäck River. In 1654, it was presented by King Karl X Gustav to his bride Hedvig Eleonora. In 1660, the year of her husband's death, the queen had the original castle torn down and asked her favorite architect, Nicodemus Tessin the Elder, to draw up plans for a new building and gardens to be fitted into this difficult site. Strömsholm stands today as a most successful monument to this collaboration, which also gave rise to Ulriksdal and Drottningholm.

Much has changed at Strömsholm since the seventeenth century. Carl Hårleman was asked in 1731 to complete the still unfinished interior. In 1774, Carl Fredrik Adelcrantz succeeded him in this task, when Gustav III gave Strömsholm as a wedding present to his bride Sofia Magdalena. The charming light chinoiserie blue dining room dates from this period. Around 1800, Tessin's wings, in which the royal family had lived during the lifetime of Hedvig Eleonora, were torn down. This subtraction from the original palace, which should have been a sacrilege, turned out to be quite a good idea. Strömsholm's central building stands very well on its own. The small surrounding formal garden and the divided river are marvelously complementary to the actual building. Strömsholm today is a palace to be lived in—light, charming, surrounded by water, and host to a score of enormous seventeenth-century animal paintings that were formerly at Gripsholm. There is also D. K. Ehrenstral's painting of the coronation of King Karl XI.

There has been a stud farm at Strömsholm since the sixteenth century and today the lovely property surrounding the palace is home to Sweden's national stud. Here beautiful bay-colored horses live freely and happily in rich pastures punctuated by apple trees. Until 1968, there was a military riding school at Strömsholm. In that year, however, the Swedish cavalry became completely mechanized. Now these horses can be seen only on special occasions and when, as part of one of Europe's last mounted military bands, they join in the trouping of the colors at Stockholm Palace.

Detail of the Chinese Salon at Strömsholm showing decorative paintings by Lars Bolander based on engravings by Pilement.

BYSTAD MANOR

Exterior view of this eighteenth-century yellow painted wooden manor house with its pavilion.

This yellow-painted wooden manor house was probably built for Baron Claes Brorsson Rålamb, who had inherited the property from his father. Rålamb was a man of many interests; his amusing tale of his trip to Constantinople in 1657 has been translated into many languages. His son Gustav Rålamb was, in the 1720s, responsible for the addition of a second story to the building, the free-standing church, and the bell tower. The property then passed through many hands before being acquired through marriage by Johan August Anckarsvärd, the agronomist. Anckarsvärd, who introduced artificial fertilizer to Sweden, made Bystad into an important agricultural center. The manor house, scheduled for destruction in 1876, was instead modernized. After restorations in 1938 and 1980, Bystad regained much of its Carolinian character.

The manor's interior riches are announced by the many-colored decorations of the columned Entrance Hall. A grisaille Hercules and his companion Apollo stand guard on either side of the doorway, while a girl in a swing, copied around 1730 from a Watteau painting, rides high above her rustic companions. On the opposite wall, a group of men and women set off to go hunting. On either side of the door leading to the Great Salon, painted trompe l'oeil checkerboard paths lead to imaginary castles. A portrait of Nils Dacke, leader of a famous peasant revolt against Gustav Vasa, hangs over a secondary doorway. From the entrance hall a double staircase rises to the first floor, where the guard rail is adorned with painted wooden statues of putti. Some of these are naked and carry garlands of flowers, others are dressed like eighteenth-century street urchins.

Bystad houses a collection of paintings that is extraordinary by any

Following page:
Entrance Hall at Bystad manor with painted tromp l'oeil checker board paths leading to imaginary castles.

standard. A watercolor of two lions signed Albrecht Dürer and dated 1512 accompanies Lucas Cranach's portrait of Luther's friend Viet Dietrich. A seventeenth century copy of a lost portrait of Gustav Vasa with a fashionable long beard, hangs in the Dining Room with another of Queen Kristina by Sebastian Bourdon. In one of the salons, Dutch painting predominates; we find drinking scenes by David Tenniers and a large painting of a pride of lions by Frans Snyders. J. Sergel's busts of Gustav III and Ulla von Hopken (sister of Axel von Fersen the Younger) stand on either side of the sofa.

Bystad manor, built on a comparatively isolated site below two large lakes, is crammed with pictorial riches worthy of any capital.

One of the carved wooden dwarfs who adorn the main staircase of Bystad manor.

Detail of panel taken from a Watteau painting around 1730.

TIDÖ CASTLE

Tidö stands free and magnificent as a monument to its builder Axel Oxenstierna the great minister of King Gustav II Adolf. Both Simon de la Vallée and Nicodemus Tessin the Elder have been credited with the construction of the building, but it would appear that the two architects were invited to participate when the chancellor's project was well under way.

To appreciate this extraordinary country palace, the visitor must know something of the man who built it. Axel Oxenstierna (1583-1654) was eleven years older than Gustav II Adolf (1594-1632), the king who, on ascending the throne, raised him to the rank of chancellor. A man as calm as his monarch was impetuous, Oxenstierna gave much attention to the construction of his various residences. Tidö castle, one of the most important among these, embodies the character of its builder. Large, well placed, and well built on dower lands brought to Oxenstierna by his wife, the castle incorporates the

The sandstone portals of Tidö were made by Heinrich Blume, a German sculptor who came to Sweden in 1621. They were carved in Stockholm and brought to Tidö complete.

The Apollo Belvedere in the garden looks towards the manor.

Tidö Castle.

Tidö, known for its inlaid wood work, has some forty-three differently carved doors made by workers from Lübeck in the seventeenth century. The portraits are of Cardinal Corsini in whose palace in Rome Queen Cristina lived, and Queen Katharina of Brandenburg consort of Christian IV of Danmark.

French and Dutch designs that the chancellor encountered while traveling abroad. Tidö's stone entrance portals were designed by Simon de la Vallée and are the work of Heinrich Blume, a German immigrant who worked in Stockholm. Oxenstierna was not satisfied with their first placement at the castle. In 1640, therefore, he had them torn down and put up again. Simon de la Vallée, a Frenchman, was also the main architect of the mansion, and Nicodemus Tessin the Elder, who was born in Pomerania, completed the gabled wings. Throughout his long years of service to the crown, Oxenstierna favored the importation of foreign talent not only in the arts but also in industry. Gustav II Adolf and Oxenstierna invited Louis de Geer and his Walloon workmen to develop Sweden's iron industry. Under Gustav II Adolf, Oxenstierna also helped to found the Swedish East India Company. In

1638, six years after the king's death, Oxenstierna, serving as regent for the minor Queen Kristina, sent Peter Minuit, who had bought Manhattan from the Indians and had been the governor of the New Netherlands from 1625 until his dismissal in 1632, with three ships of settlers across the Atlantic to establish the colony of "New Sweden" in America's faraway Delaware Valley. This colony did not last long. In 1665, it was swallowed by New Netherlands which, in turn, was gobbled up by the British colonies. Domestically, Oxenstierna's commercial policies brought an era of prosperity to his fellow countrymen. During the minority of Queen Kristina, he became known as Sweden's "uncrowned king." Later, at Westphalia in 1648, he was instrumental in achieving an advantageous settlement for his country. As the queen grew older, however, she quarreled with her minister over her plans

The Winter Salon with its painted panels from Axel Oxenstierna's time, while the grisaille painted ceiling is from the end of the seventeenth century.

Tidö Castle.
View from the Billiard Room towards
the Blue Gustavian Dining Room.
Detail of the stove in the Billiard
Room. Its flowered decoration is a
typical pattern of the day. The figure is
one of a pair of French empire
lacquered bronze putti.

This door illustrates the Gustavian
spirit that dominates the Blue Dining
Room.

for the royal succession and Oxenstierna spent more and more time in semiretirement at Tidö. A firm Lutheran, he was deeply upset by Kristina's determination to convert to Catholicism and reside abroad. He died in 1654, a few months after her abdication. Work at Tidö had commenced in 1620, but the castle was still unfinished at the time of its master's death. Even today, a large room on the uppermost floor that may have been intended as a meeting hall stands empty, awaiting its role. Oxenstierna's interest in furnishing his castle can be seen in the famous forty-three wooden doors that embellish Tidö's state apartment. These doors, one of which is in the Swedish National Museum in Stockholm, are tall, ornate, enriched with sculpture, and inlaid with contrasting wood. No two doors are alike; each attests the perfectionism of the cabinet-makers from Lübeck who created them.

The furnishings of the state apartments date from the seventeenth century. Above the large open fireplace in the Manorial Hall, Axel Oxenstierna's coat of arms and that of his wife are carved with the date 1652, but most of the furniture dates from the day of his grandson, Carl Gustav Oxenstierna. The grandfather clock is of particular interest. Dated 1684, it came to Tidö via the widow of Otto Wilhelm von Koenigsmarck, a professional soldier. (Koenigsmarck was commander of the besieging Venetian forces in 1684, when the gunpowder stored by the Turks in the Parthenon exploded and partially destroyed that faraway structure.) His armorial canopy is flanked by portraits of Axel Oxenstierna and his wife; some of their descendants populate the other walls of the imposing hall.

The Gustavian rooms surrounding the Oxenstierna apartments were retouched and redecorated throughout the nineteenth century. The Yellow Drawing Room was rearranged as late as 1910. These rooms are light and colorful; most of their furniture is from the eighteenth century. In the Yellow Drawing Room there is a charming double portrait of Gustav III and his son, painted in about 1790 by Jonas Forslund. A Swedish copy of Titian's *Danae* occupies the place of honor. The Long Gallery, which was also redecorated at the turn of the century, is furnished in the same style as the Yellow Drawing Room and the Blue Dining Room. Here we find three neoclassic marble busts, a statue of Ganymede, and another of a lady arranging her hair. There are Dutch paintings grouped around an equestrian portrait of Karl XII and two porphyry vases from Karl XIV Johan's porphyry works at Älvdalen.

In the castle's large dining room, Empire and Victorian furniture and decoration merge. Of particular interest is the large, formal gilded bronze French table setting given to Tidö's owner by Karl XIV Johan.

Decoration in the Billiard Room is almost entirely Empire and of particular importance is this monumental Swedish desk.

A rococo cabinet and the Billiard Room complete this large suite of rooms. In the latter, a collection of nineteenth-century portraits of the Von Schinkel family, Tidö's present owners, faces the busts of the Emperor Napoleon and Karl Friedrich Schinkel, the German architect. Tidö has two libraries containing thousands of seventeenth- and eighteenth-century volumes, medieval manuscripts, and even an illuminated seventeenth-century manuscript of the Koran. An entailed property since 1890, the castle is always being enriched by its owners. Currently Captain Carl David von Schinkel is still expanding the enormous and fascinating toy museum that he has established in one of the wings. Galleries on two floors illustrate the development of childrens' toys made for the Swedish market from the eighteenth century to the

Tidö Castle.
Two of the 2,500 toys gathered in Tidö's magnificent toy museum.

modern era. The museum, which was opened to the public on June 17, 1974, by King Carl XVI Gustaf, has never stopped growing. Every imaginable china doll, teddy bear, hand puppet, wind-up toy, child-sized racing car, lead soldier, and model battleship is at home in a suitable habitat with hundreds of its own kind. The most casual visitor becomes an instant toy fanatic, eager to spend hours studying the infinite variety of the collection. There is even a miniature bakery shop and a medieval torture chamber.

The park around Tidö is home to cast-iron gods and an oak tree said to have been planted by Axel Oxenstierna. Apollo Belvedere is ensconced in the baroque garden to the east of the castle. To the west, the English park blends into the neat meadows and buttery fields of

the working farms surrounding the property. There are still many half-tamed deer in Tidö's woods. On misty mornings, these sometimes greet visitors at the garden's edge.

Tidö castle today is golden, handsome, well maintained, and impressive—just as Axel Oxenstierna would have wished it to be.

The larger library contains rare documents, manuscripts, seventeenth and eighteenth-century volumes, and two globes by Anders Åkerman.

FULLERÖ MANOR

The manor at Fullerö—a timbered dwelling of simple proportions is probably the work of Jean de la Vallée. It is a copy in wood of the House of Nobility in Stockholm, most of which was designed by Jean's father, Simon de la Vallée.

The manor house at Fullerö—a timbered dwelling of simple proportions, is probably the work of Jean de la Vallée. It is a miniature copy in wood of the House of Nobility in Stockholm, which was largely designed by Jean's father, Simon de la Vallée. Two distinguishing marks of a gentleman owner are found in the architecture of this seventeenth-century manor house, the raised or *säteri* roof and the painted wooden exterior. In the seventeenth century, farmhouses had

an unpainted, weatherbeaten look, but the houses of the gentry were, like Fullerö, generally painted "Falu red," a color that was the result of a process first undertaken at the Falun copper mine. During the eighteenth century, the nobility started painting their houses yellow, while Falu red found favor with the lower classes.

Curiously, it was at Fullerö that the closed stove replaced the open fireplace. In response to a royal order to conserve forests, Count Carl Johan Cronstedt and General Fabian Wrede invented the tubular stove and installed several here as an experiment.

One of the linden alleys leading to Fullerö manor house.

Detail of the roof lines of the pavilion and main house, showing another aspect of the säteri or raised roof line.

ENGSÖ CASTLE

A painting at Engsö castle of the building as it appeared after the reconstruction in 1740.

Engsö, first mentioned in twelfth-century royal documents, has always been treasured by its inhabitants. From 1307 until 1710, the property belonged to succeeding branches of the Sparre family. In about 1480, Bengt Fadersson Sparre built at Engsö "a firm house of stone" over the prison and cellar of the building. This "house" was enlarged in 1630 and became the mansion pictured on these pages and in Eric Dahlberg's *Svecia Antiqua et Hodierna*. Until 1691, the proprietors of Engsö castle enjoyed the power of life and death over the inhabitants of the estate. Not even the King could veto the "Engsö

First mentioned as a castle in a royal parchment letter of the twelvth century, Engsö was rebuilt as a manor house

A view of the noted fourteenth century chapel at Engsö.

Neck and Hand Court," and the dungeon of the castle was filled until Karl XI rescinded the estate's privileges. Johan Sigismund Sparre, the proprietor who reluctantly accepted this decree, also enjoyed another distinction. Legend has it that one dark night Sparre played dice with the devil and won a gold chain, five feet in length, which is still on exhibit in Engsö castle, as is the Renaissance portrait of Brita Baat, a hard-hearted woman who, having been widowed twice, married a third time, only to be driven from Engsö church by the ghosts of her former husbands. In 1710 the property was acquired by the Piper

Engsö Castle.

Eighteenth-century mural painting in the reception hall of Engsö castle.

family, who established an entail, stipulating that Engsö could no longer be sold or divided. As a result, the property was enriched throughout the eighteenth century.

During the early 1700s, Carl Hårleman, one of the finest architects of the time, added a fourth story to the main structure and designed two well-proportioned, detached wings to flank the castle. Since the interior was also redecorated at this time, the rooms and galleries almost without exception reflect the rococo style of the mid-eighteenth century. Many charming examples of trompe l'oeil are scattered throughout the castle, including the niche in the rococo salon holding a bust of Karl XII and, in the count's cabinet, the blue canvas wall covering made to imitate damask. At the end of the century, Countess Sophie Piper, born von Fersen, illegally stripped Engsö of many treasures in order to pay her gambling debts. The collection of family portraits, however, remains in the castle today.

Engsö church is fascinating in its own right. Although the tower and the funerary chapel were added in 1740, the church proper is medieval and adorned with paintings (since restored) dating from the mid-fourteenth century. Fifty-two carved and painted coats of arms hang on the walls and a medieval statue of Saint Anne in polychrome wood stands in the vestry. The seated saint hold the Blessed Virgin on her lap and she, in turn, is holding the child Jesus up for worship. To the left of the castle and above the Hårleman wings stands a dwelling built in the 1760s by Fredrik Wilhelm Hoppe. Here members of the Piper family live to this day. Although the entail has now come to an end, the Engsö estate is still intact and functions as a working farm.

Engsö castle stands surrounded by rich grain fields. These fields, dotted with outcroppings of glacial granite, are testimony not only to their farmers' tenacity but also to winters of unimaginable ferocity. In 1733, in fact, Anders Åhman, an estate foreman, complained that the local wolves had become so starved that they snatched his water dog from between his legs and devoured it on the spot.

GRÖNSÖÖ CASTLE

Placed on what was an island, the manor house at Grönsöö was built for Gustav II Adolf's teacher Johan Skytte in the early years of the seventeenth century.

The Chinese Pavilion at the water's edge is of particular interest. Evocations of Chinese art and architecture appeared throughout Europe during the eighteenth century, and this pavilion, like the one in Drottningholm, is a manifestation of that fashion. The wooden structure, complete with curved roof line and pagoda elements, has an interior decorated with shells. It faces the original manor house, which stands across the water on the opposite bank of lake Mälaren.

The Chinese pavilion stands on the opposite shore to the Grönsöö castle.

RYDBOHOLM CASTLE

The Vasa Tower, a mid-fifteenth-century building, property of the father of Gustav Vasa, has been shortened in the seventeenth century by one story from its original size.

Rydboholm Castle is just north of Stockholm, and legend has it that King Gustav Vasa was born there in 1496. At the time of his birth, Rydboholm was the property of his father, Erik Johansson, a leader of the Swedish nobility, who was murdered by the Danes in 1520. Although the tale that he was born there cannot be verified, it is certain that young Gustav Eriksson spent much of his youth at Rydboholm, living to the rhythm of sowing and reaping. Indeed he formalized this agricultural year by edict after his accession (1523) to the throne. Hay had to be in by St. Olof's Day (July 29) and grain by St. Bartholomew's (August 24); moreover, church and social functions were curtailed during planting and harvest and farmers who neglected their fields would find their property taken over by the crown. Not least among

Detail of window in the tower at Rydboholm.

the nobles who tried to emulate the king's devotion to the land was his nephew Per Brahe, Gustav Vasa's sister Margareta's son and Rydboholm's new master. A thrifty, knowledgeable farmer, Brahe became Sweden's first count and richest private landowner. In 1581, seated in what is today called Gustav Vasa's study, Brahe composed a treatise entitled *Oeconomia*—"a household book for noble folk"—so as to pass his principles of piety, self-respect, and caution on to future generations. His formula proved successful with regard to his own descendants. The burial of the last Brahe owner of Rydboholm took place in 1930 (after which Nathan Söderblom, the archbishop, locked the Brahe crypt in the nearby medieval church at Östra Ryd and threw the key into the river). For 500 years, the family had periodically refurbished the estate, although Rydboholm was not always their principal home. (Nils Brahe, 1632-1699, married Margareta Juliana Wrangel, daughter of Field Marshall Karl Gustaf Wrangel who was heiress to Skokloster Castle and many other estates.) The Brahes carefully preserved the freestanding medieval Vasa Tower and the castle built to complement it. The tower, which is open to the public, is of particular interest. The exact date of its construction (sometime in the fifteenth century) is unknown, but its rooms were paneled and painted in the mid-sixteenth century. These paintings faded by time, match those of Kalmar and Gripsholm in quality. Probably executed by Dutch artists inspired by the school of Fontainbleau, they depict farms, fruit, wines, musical instruments, and both real and imaginary figures.

Rydboholm Castle.
Birgitta's chamber, named after Brita Sture, is the only room whose decorations date from the sixteenth century. The trees, painted directly on the plaster, are reminiscent of verdure tapestries.

A portrait of Margareta Vasa dated 1528 hangs on one study wall. Now one story shorter than when it was built, the tower stands at the water's edge. The oldest wing of the castle, just behind it, also dates from Vasa days. The trees on the walls of Birgitta's chamber may have been painted in the sixteenth century or at the end of the seventeenth. Experts disagree on the subject.

Since Rydboholm has never been sold, all of the castle's contents are of interest as an inventory of Swedish domestic history. Among the paintings, that by C. W. von Brede depicting a scene from Gustav III's drama *The Valor of Gustav Adolf* is of particular importance, as is the one showing Gustav II Adolf at Ebba Brahe's wedding.

Older even than the paneled paintings in the Vasa Tower are the decorations gracing the walls and ceilings of Östra Ryd Church. These, dated 1449, are the work of Johannes Ivan. The park at Rydboholm contains two oak trees allegedly planted by Gustav Vasa.

Legend has it that Gustav Vasa was born in this room in the Vasa Tower. The panels are from 1550, they were probably installed when the study was redecorated for Gustav Vasa's nephew, Count Per Brahe the Elder.

ROSERSBERG PALACE

Delineatio Splendidissimi Palatii ROSERSBERG   abeaparte quæ hortum Spect

W. Swidde Sculp: Holmiæ 1695.

Willem Swidde's engraving from Svecia
Antiqua et Hodierna *of the castle
and two details of the garden.*

*This fourteenth-century castle was
rebuilt in 1630, after having changed
hands many times and is now a military
establishment.*

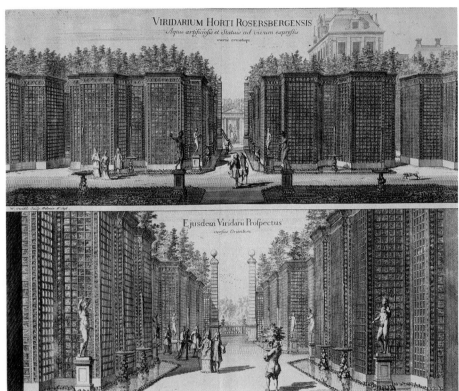

VIRIDARIUM HORTI ROSERSBERGENSIS
Aquis artificiosis et Statuis ad vivum expressis varie ornatum

Ejusdem Viridarii Prospectus
versus Orientem

Rosersberg Palace today is quite different from what it was in 1613, when Gabriel Bengtsson Oxenstierna named this property in honor of the three roses on his mother's familial coat of arms. Since that time there have been many additions and alterations. The old engraving in Erik Dahlberg's *Svecia Antiqua et Hodierna* shows a building with three floors as well as three wings linked to the main building by simple portals. The main entrance was marked by a very tall tower. When Bengt Gabrielsson Oxenstierna bought Rosersberg in 1682, he commissioned Nicodemus Tessin the Younger to adjust and refinish it in the French neobaroque manner.

Rosersberg Castle.
Exterior staircase to the garden.
Rosersberg was given its name by
Gabriel Begtsson Oxenstierna to honor
his mother Sigrid "Tre Rosor."

Two new wings with lanterned, roofed pavilions were added. Grottoes were created in their basements, and these became cool summer rooms connecting the castle with the greatly enlarged gardens. Under Oxenstierna, Rosersberg was the center of one of the largest baroque parks in the country. The old garden, punctuated with statues, became a huge formal parterre. A dam was built sixty meters east of the castle so that the fountains might be well supplied, and a gazebo made entirely of tile became the site of afternoon gatherings. Unfortunately, much of baroque Rosersberg was plastered over when Baron Erland Broman bought the property in 1747. Only Tessin's East Gallery was spared, ultimately to become the palace chapel. Otherwise, we know the older version of the palace only from books and engravings.

Erland Broman, a favorite of both King Fredrik I and King Adolf Fredrik, called in Jean Eric Rehn to bring the buildings up to date.

When the property was sold to the crown, work was suspended; but in 1762 it was passed to Prince Karl, Fredrik Adolf's second son, who later became duke of Södermanland (1772) and King Karl XIII (1809-1818). Since it was not a royal property, Rosersberg had to be refurbished so as to be worthy of its owners. After 1770, Duke Karl had Rehn brought back several times to develop and refurbish apartments of state in the palace. Rosersberg's exterior was altered to accomodate new windows, and wings were added.

On Duke Karl's marriage to Hedvig Elisabet Charlotta of Oldenburg in 1774, the new duchess was provided with both state and small apartments on the west side of the palace, while her ladies in waiting were lodged in the west wing and the duke's attendants in the old palace church. It was now that Tessin's gallery became the duke's chapel. During Gustav III's lifetime, his brother did not dispose of much money, so the duke's large reception suite was not created until 1797. Then, Gustav af Sillén designed the third-floor library, with its spiral staircase down to the duke's bedroom (1799); the cabinet room; and the Högland Salon, commemorating the duke's career as grand admiral during the 1788-1790 war against Russia. Here we see Duke Karl's love of symbolism. The walls, stuccoed to resemble marble, support painted "triumphs" of antique armor. A grisaille frieze of battle scenes runs around the room, above twelve marble medallions showing Gustav III, Duke Karl, and the Swedish commanders of the war. Above this is another frieze of ducal crowns and crosses. L. J. Desprez's huge painting of the battle of Högland occupies almost the whole interior wall, while the blue and yellow curtains framing the windows echo the Swedish flag. It is a room whose every detail proclaims the hero.

Rosersberg Castle.
Library entrance, an important example of Karl XIII classicism designed by Gustav af Sillén.

Unfortunately the duke, unlike his elder brother (who wintered on the royal yacht in the Baltic to be near his troops), had little taste for hardship. His battles were won by his subordinates, who considered him a shirker. The martial symbolism of the Högland Salon is a parade of fictions. A lifetime Mason, Duke Karl became head of Swedish Freemasonry on the death of Gustav III. His wife was also very interested in the movement; her lovely state bedchamber abounds with stars, cubes, circles, and flames, all reflecting Masonic liturgy. Frederik Westin's overdoor paintings of Night, Dawn, Noon, and Evening might have been taken from Mozart's *Magic Flute.* They were done for Queen Hedvig Elisabet Charlotte in 1813, later to be complemented by the same artist's *Four Seasons,* commissioned by Queen Desirée in 1823. The Bernardotte monarchs did nothing to alter the Masonic symbols found at Rosersberg. Indeed, a footnote in the official guide to the queen's state bedchamber hints at a connection between "the Polaris of the Mariner—the cynosure that guides the Masons over the stormy seas of time—the seven stars are the symbol of right and justice to the order and the nation" and the starry coat of arms Napoleon's field marshal had created for his family when he became Sweden's crown prince.

In the era that saw the orphaned Lafayette welcomed by Washington as a spiritual son and fellow Freemason, when Benjamin Franklin was inducted by the duke of Chartres into France's most important Masonic Lodge, Freemasonry may well have served as a link between those seeking a fit heir for Sweden's childless king and his actual successor. Bernardotte was not an obvious choice; However, if his worth was known to a whole network of initiates, then it is understandable that he established himself with ease in a markedly foreign nation. In any case, at Rosersberg the Masonic symbols are still in place and Duke Karl's chapel is unaltered to this day. A long rectangle with a double enfilade of thirty-two columns leads to a slightly raised sanctuary; this is a cube decorated with stars and circles; it is crowned by a domed ceiling centered on a painted sun. The chapel is today a perfect place for ceremonies in which petitioners are led from darkness to light, from ignorance to knowledge. But does it not date from 1695? Isn't it Tessin's gallery frescoed by Giuseppe Marchi, open to daylight on three sides? Yes, but windows can be covered, sanctuaries veiled, candelabras extinguished—only to be lit again by the light of new truths.

It would be wrong to think of Karl XIII as a man of illuminated intelligence. Although he was influenced by the age of reason, he could be extremely credulous and superstitious. In his early youth, he had been told by a fortune teller that he would be king, so he spent his whole life conspiring toward that end. First he plotted against his brother Gustav III, who never allowed himself to believe the evidence of Duke Karl's repeated betrayals; then he schemed successfully against his nephew Gustav IV Adolf.

Caught between two great reigns, Karl XIII cuts a sorry figure in Swedish history—everywhere except at Rosersberg. Here the shirker can pose as hero and the conspirator assume the airs of the monarch. Duke Karl had good taste in furniture, and the neoclassical rooms designed for him by Gustav af Sillén mark a beautiful transition from the pure Gustavian to the Karl XIV Johan style as seen in Rosendal.

Karl XIII also built a pseudo ruin in Rosersberg's English Park to house his huntsmen, as well as a hermitage that was home to an ornamental hermit. These monuments have unfortunately been destroyed, but they can still be seen in contemporary paintings. Queen Desirée brought her engraved copy of the American Declaration of Independence to Rosersberg.

Karl XIV Johan invited Frederik Blom to renew the royal apartments in the spirit of Rosendal. The furnishings and decorations of the king's green silk bedroom are taken from French Empire designs by Perciere and Fontaine of Paris. The king's bed is placed within a columned alcove, his desk is a pedestal, and his stove is a white column. The ceiling is circled with stars.

King Karl XIV Johan's bedroom designed by Fredrik Blom in 1823, is one of the best examples of French empire imported and adopted in Sweden.

STENINGE MANOR

Tessin the Younger finished the baroque italianate manor house at Steninge in 1698 for Carl Gyllenstierna. The site is composed of the main building, two pavilions and a number of smaller red painted wood buildings and a lovely Italian garden on both sides of the house. It was built at the lake Mälaren for both aesthetic and practical reasons as the waterways provided easy access to the capital in all seasons.

This "marvelous and unusual jewel" was built for Carl Gyllenstierna by Nicodemus Tessin the Younger in the last decade of the seventeenth century. It still looks almost exactly as it did when Erik Dahlbergh made a drawing of it for *Svecia Antiqua et Hodierna* in 1695, even though the house was not completed until 1699.

Gyllenstierna, who had inherited the property from his mother in 1669, took his time about creating a perfect setting for the visits of his great patron the widowed Queen Hedvig Eleonora, whom he had met in 1668 when he was eighteen and she thirty-two.

Nicodemus Tessin the Elder had been the first architect approached to replace the wood manor that had formerly stood on the property. But the queen and her protegé found his designs old-fashioned and procrastinated until after his death in 1681. Then they had to wait for Tessin the Younger's return from his foreign travels. He finally set to work, assisted by workmen from Dalecarlia taken from other royal projects and, on the queen's orders, the Uppland Regiment. These soldiers helped to complete the stone terraces supporting the manor's entrances and the square, freestanding wings. The stone buildings were and are a lovely rosy peach color with white columns and trim. The two older wooden wings, somewhat downhill between the mansion and the water, are painted bright red. These served respectively as bakery and sauna. In June 1702, Tessin and Johan Hårleman—who had designed Steninge's garden, with its sphinx alleyways, urns, grottoes, and friezes—came with their wives and servants to inspect the project. (Tessin was so pleased that, from then on, he used his drawings of Steninge as samples to attract other patrons.) August 1705 saw the official housewarming, which was attended by the dowager queen and Hårleman and commemorated by a specially made service of glassware, whose pieces can still be found in various museums throughout Sweden. Gyllenstierna married in 1706 and gave Steninge to his bride, a rich widow named Anna Maria Soop, as a "morning gift." She entailed and maintained the property, leaving it upon her death to her daughter by a previous marriage. This daughter married into the Fersen family, so that Steninge became, in 1794, the property of Axel von Fersen the Younger, one of the most romantic figures of Swedish history.

This monument to Axel von Fersen in the garden was designed by Olof Tempelman.

Fersen, like Gyllenstierna, was fated to be linked to a ruling queen, but there all resemblance ends. Steninge's founder prospered as governor of Hedvig Eleonora's household and manager of her estates. What better way to build a beautiful country home than with the support and advice of the country's prime builder? Steninge's queen's wing was stuccoed by Giuseppe Marchi, a royal craftsman. The manor's ornately carved and gilded oval salon reflects the queen's preference for the baroque. Everywhere throughout the property, Hedvig Eleonora's benevolent and enriching presence is felt. After her death in 1715, Gyllenstierna lived on in comfort at Steninge until his own demise in 1723.

Fersen's association with royalty was destined to conclude less happily. When he met Marie Antoinette on January 10, 1774, she was dauphiness of France, while he was a young nobleman completing an obligatory "grand tour." They were both nineteen. The unhappily married Austrian-born princess made no secret of her admiration of the visiting Swede, flirting openly with him at a masked ball at the Paris Opera. Fersen left Paris on May 12 of that year, only two days after the death of Louis XV, making Marie Antoinette and her husband, Louis XVI, the rulers of France.

He then returned to France to volunteer, with the Swedish king's permission, for service with the French expeditionary forces in North America. In America, he served so efficiently as the marquis de Rochambeau's aide-de-champ that George Washington offered him the order of Cincinnatus, but Gustav III did not allow his officer to wear this revolutionary decoration. By 1783 "Le Beau Fersen," thanks again to Gustav III, was back at Versailles—this time as the proprietary colonel of the French king's Royal Swedish Regiment. He stayed close to the French royal couple until the night of June 20, 1791, when, following Louis XVI's orders, he left them on the road to Varennes. After their forced return and imprisonment, Fersen never stopped trying to free them; but Louis XVI was guillotined in January 1793. Fersen then returned several times at the risk of his life to try to free Marie Antoinette, but in vain. She was executed on October 16, 1793, leaving the curious to speculate about the nature of her attachment to the taciturn Swede.

Fersen altered and edited most of the notes Marie Antoinette had managed to send him from prison. His family destroyed all other correspondence that they considered indiscreet. Then, in the 1930s, Oscar von Heidenstam remembered how close Fersen had been to Sophie Piper, his sister, a series of heartbreaking letters written by Fersen were found in the archives of Löfstad Castle. Here is part of one dated August 24, 1793, when the queen was imprisoned in the Conciergerie: " . . . If I could yet do something towards her deliverance, I think I should suffer less. . . . Oh, the horror of having to wait without doing anything. I would give my life to save her and I am unable to do it! My greatest happiness would be to die for her, and that happiness is refused me. Oh, if only cowardly ruffians had not deprived me of the best of kings. How I feel all the extent of my loss at this moment! He alone would have been capable of saving her. His great soul would have been fired with the story of her ills, and he would have dared everything to come to help. But he is no more and the last hope dies with him. Adieu, my dear Sophie. Pray to God for her, and pity your unhappy brother." (The reference is to Gustav III, who had throughout the years become more and more friendly with the French queen.) Fersen's devotion to the queen of France influenced every aspect of his life long after her death. The young officer who had served with Washington became the bitterest of reactionaries. His hatred of anything that smacked of revolution was absolute. He was thought to be the evil genius who inspired Gustav III's rigid and authoritarian son Gustav IV Adolf. When this king was deposed in 1809, Fersen withdrew from politics but remained grand marshal of the nobility. On May 28, 1810, the newly selected heir to the throne died of apoplexy. An unfounded rumor started that Fersen had had the man poisoned. On June 20, 1810, Fersen, who was to have led the funeral procession, was pulled from his carriage, chased through the streets of Stockholm, and torn to pieces by a mob howling for blood.

In the English park at Steninge, a Gothic-style monument erected by Fersen's brother in 1813 bears an inscription extolling Axel von Fersen's virtues and mourning his fate. The monument is by Olof Tempelman, the decoration by E. G. Gothe, and the inscription by J. O. Wallin. Within the manor, a gilded Sèvres coffee set is lovingly preserved in a special display table. It was a gift to Fersen from Marie Antoinette.

Steninge Manor.
A red clocktower in the garden.

Opposite page:
One of Sweden's grand baroque rooms, designed by Tessin the Younger in the 1690s and restored in 1912. The statues in the room are nineteenth-century Italian.

SKOKLOSTER CASTLE

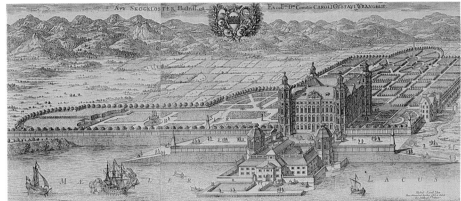

Carl Gustaf Wrangel comissioned the German architect Caspar Vogel to design a castle which had to prove the power and richness of the Wrangels both in Sweden and in Pomerania. Nicodemus Tessin the Younger and Jean de la Vallée are also supposed to have worked on this project. Construction of the building began in 1654. Four octagonal towers complete the angle of each facade.

Engraving of Skokloster from E. Dahlbergh. "Svecia Antiqua et Hodierna."

Skokloster Castle.
The grandious King's Hall with gilt leather wall covering is filled with portraits of kings from Gustav Vasa to Gustav VI Adolf.

Opposite page:
Countess Wrangel's bedroom with her monumental red silk damask gold paielleted bed. The walls are covered with tapestries from Gouda in Holland.

Skokloster's four octagonal towers seem to rise from the waters of Lake Mälaren. This castle lies north of Stockholm and can be reached from the capital by either land or water. For centuries the latter was the preferred route, as the waterways froze solid in winter and travel by sleigh was fairly easy. Skokloster is unique among Swedish castles in that it exists for itself. Unencumbered by dependent villages, it stands today as a monument to its builder's pride. Carl Gustaf Wrangel (1613-1676) was born at Skokloster, the son of Herman Wrangel, a Lithuanian nobleman, who made his way up through the wars of Swedish expansion and was named field marshal in 1638. After his father's death in 1643, Carl Gustaf felt himself free to transform this property (inherited from his mother Margareta Grip) into a residence resembling to the North German castles he had come to admire during his years of service with the Swedish army abroad. While his huge white castle grew toward the heavens, Wrangel inhabited the *casa canonica*, which had once served as the rectory of the Cistercian convent and in which he had been born. Work began on the castle foundation in 1654, but the interior of the banqueting hall was still unfinished at the time of Wrangel's death. Carl Gustaf Wrangel, who served bril-

Skokloster Castle.
Lathe room containing the seventeenth-century wood working instruments used by Carl Gustaf Wrangel and Nils Brahe.

liantly and successfully under four Swedish monarchs, was a man who knew what he wanted. There is a model of the castle at Skokloster, made by Barthel Volkland in Pomerania in 1657. It can be taken apart, and when this is done, the four separate stories appear almost exactly as their actual counterparts do today. From this, it can be deduced that although Wrangel consulted both Nicodemus Tessin the Elder and Jean de la Vallée, he was actually his own architect, relying ultimately on plans drawn up for him by Caspar Vogel of Erfurt and his own impressions of Aschaffenburg Castle on the Main River, which he and Turenne had captured in 1646. Wrangel liked the pomp and power of these German structures, as is evident from the models and engravings of his ten other castles on display at Skokloster. Most of these are multistoried and large. But Skokloster was Wrangel's prime residence and his principal statement of self; on his death, it passed to his eldest daughter who, in 1701, entailed the property in her father's memory.

Because she had married into the Brahe family and her son married a Bielke heiress, Skokloster's collections were greatly enriched by various inheritances. There are three armories at Skokloster, the most important being that of Wrangel himself. He collected 750 hunting guns and 150 pistols; all are on display in rooms especially designed for this purpose. Also on display are Polish and Turkish sabers, costumes from the coronation of Karl X Gustav in 1654 (the oldest known Swedish theatrical costumes), and a sachem's paraphernalia from the Swedish colony in North America. The Brahe and Bielke armories were assembled over the generations; the latter contains a fine selection of Swedish flintlock guns and several Turkish tents, saddles, and harnesses captured in Hungary in 1687.

The libraries of the Wrangel, Brahe, Bielke, and Scheffer families—almost 20,000 volumes of documents from the fifteenth to the eighteenth centuries—are gathered in seven rooms on the east side of Skokloster's fourth floor. The rooms themselves are very handsome, with white walls and ceilings decorated with festoons of flowers. These, original to the building, were restored in the 1830s. Carl Gustaf Wrangel, like many of his contemporaries, enjoyed doing woodwork. His collection of lathes is now displayed in a tower room, which also houses tools used by Nils Brahe and Gabriel Oxenstierna. Many other collections may be seen in Skokloster's more than two hundred rooms. Linens, glass, paintings, tapestries, and assorted "loot" fill the castle to its attics. All illustrate Wrangel's love of grandeur. He collected paintings by the yard, paying less for a Cranach than for the portrait of a field marshal. More than anything, he loved portraits of himself, his family, and his generals. It was he who introduced David Klöker, an artist from Hamburg, to Sweden, where he was taken up by the royal family and ennobled by Queen Hedvig Eleonora as David Klocker Ehrenstrahl.

Detail from the ceiling in the King's Hall representing America. The ceiling was made in high relief colored stucco with the central image showing Sweden extending its influence to the four continents.

Ehrenstal's equestrian portrait of Carl Gustav Wrangel is the first large equestrian portrait of a nonroyal personage in Swedish history. Another portrait of Wrangel is equally significant, shown at the age of six, in a pose imitating those of his father's generals.

There is little of the eighteenth century in Skokloster. All is power and impressiveness, recalling the days of Sweden's north European empire. Rooms upon rooms have stuccoed ceilings and tapestried walls, while silver-gilt leather adorns the sleeping alcoves and sequined damask drapes the beds of the state. These played so important a role in the decoration of this cold, drafty castle, where all the state rooms except the countess's bedroom have marble floors. When Wrangel received King Karl XI in 1672, the guest rooms were packed with more than a hundred opulent four-poster beds, occupied by between two and four hundred guests. Throughout the castle, there are dozens of chests brought back from Denmark, mountains of North German armor, even a pair of Archimbaldo paintings from Prague. It should be noted that the six beautiful Brussels tapestries illustrating the life of Alexander the Great were the gift of Louis XIV to Nils Bielke, who gave them to his grandson rather than selling them to the Swedish crown. In the first half of the nineteenth century, Magnus Brahe recreated certain of Skokloster's rooms to approximate the originals as shown in illustrations. He also fleshed out the collections and built a Bernadotte monument in one of the tower rooms to honor King Karl XIV Johan, whom he served as official French-Swedish translator throughout his reign. Here a rather small octagonal chamber is dominated by a huge, scantily draped marble statue of the monarch as Mars; its size is emphasized by two more modest marble statues of the king in modern dress. The Italian diplomat Lorenzo Magalotti described the count at the summit of his success as "tall, attractive . . . proud . . . well mannered . . . and very susceptible to women. . . ." Magalotti went on to add that "with all this his residence has the appearance of belonging not to a distinguished gentleman but to a German prince." One cannot help feeling that Wrangel would have considered this description a compliment.

HAMMARBY, LINNAEUS MANOR

A small manor house acquired by Carolus Linaeus in 1762. The house originally consisted of a turf-roofed one story building. To this sanctuary men of science came from all over Europe to pay homage to the greatest naturalist of his day.

This red-painted wooden house with two barnlike, detached wings hardly deserves to be called a manor, yet it was the summer home of one of the eighteenth century's greatest scientists. Carolus Linnaeus (1707-1778) built Hammarby on land he purchased near Uppsala in 1758.

Furnished with the scanty symbols of his newly acquired nobility—a gilt pier mirror, a pendulum clock, and portraits of his sovereigns, parents, wife, son, and four daughters—Hammarby was Linnaeus's castle; as such, it was dedicated to his all-consuming love of science. Two of the most interesting pictures preserved here are the portrait of Grinn, a monkey sent to him as present by Queen Lovisa Ulrika, and a drawing of Sjupp, the first raccoon ever to arrive in Sweden and also a gift from the king. (Sjupp lived happily with the professor for almost a year, until the day he jumped over a wall and was killed by a dog.) Linnaeus was as proud of his country seat as of his professorship and his admission (in 1761) into the Order of the Polar Star. On a hill behind the simple manor house Linnaeus built a tiny museum to house his painstakingly gathered botanical and zoological collections. Here he would hold outdoor symposiums for students not only from Uppsala but from all over Europe. From here he would lead his followers on nature walks, during which they would gather and classify the plants to be found in the surrounding woods and meadows. The paths Linnaeus followed are maintained to the present day, and modern students can still feel that they are treading in the footsteps of the father of botany. For Linnaeus was the greatest of naturalists—a man who took on the task of making the order of nature understandable to his fellow men. Today his classifications have been superseded and many of his conclusions disproved. However, in establishing his theories of the relationships between (and within) species and confirming the sexuality of plants, Linnaeus taught generations of scientists how to see. To Leonardo da Vinci, the words *saper vedere* (to know how to see) marked the starting point of all art and all science. That is why

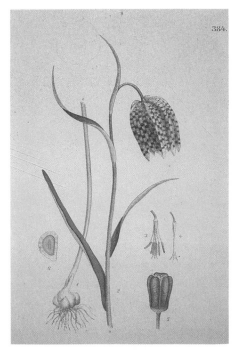

Engraving by Carl Fredrik Akrell.

Kingspasture—Kungängslilja—a flower native to Uppland which grows plentifully in Hammarby's garden.

Leonardo considered vision the most important of the senses. Equipped only with a magnifying glass, Linnaeus went out and looked at the natural world as few other scientists had done before. He saw order rather than chaos and patterns rather than anecdotes.

Linnaeus's first great patron was Carl Tessin, who offered the penniless scientist a room in his Stockholm house and a "free fork" at his table. Tessin introduced Linnaeus at court and Queen Lovisa Ulrika made him especially welcome. Gruff, pedantic, snobbish to the point of silliness (he wore his knight's cross at all times, even on field trips), Linnaeus was also something of a domestic tyrant. He would not allow his daughters either to learn French or to visit the court, and he found all the girls whom his son wished to marry unsuitable. After his death, his widow sold his collections and retired with three unmarried daughters to live summer and winter at Hammarby in genteel poverty. The winters must have been rather lonely, but in summer the small garden laid out by Linnaeus was a scented bower. This garden has been faithfully reproduced, complete with plants from Lapland and Siberia. Today, even the hastiest visitor cannot but pause, study the plants' "Linnaean" name tags, look out over the surrounding plain, and see the world as Linnaeus saw it.

SALSTA CASTLE

Although modeled on Vaux-le-Vicomte, Salsta has its origins in a medieval castle. Constructed in the heart of Uppland forest, the building is particularly Swedish in that the master bedrooms are situated on the first and not on the main floor of the manor.

Between 1577 and 1777, when Salsta Castle belonged to the Bielke family, the building was twice transformed. (The earlier castle is depicted in three engravings made by Willem Swidde for Eric Dahlberg's *Svecia Antiqua et Hodierna*.)

The present building was commissioned by Nils Bielke (1644-1716), who served from 1679 to 1682 as Swedish ambassador to the court of Louis XIV. The French monarch liked Bielke and gave him the beautiful "Alexander" tapestries that are now in Skokloster. Serving as ambassador, Bielke also obtained an extraordinarily handsome suite of

Engraving by Willem Swidde from Svecia Antiqua et Hodierna.

French gilded baroque furniture, now in Stockholm's art museum. Salsta, adorned with double wings and a double staircase, was rebuilt around a large courtyard by Mathias Spihler, who had been a pupil of Nicodemus Tessin the Elder. Tessin's plans for the building are still in existence at Skokloster; they correspond closely with the completed castle, which also owes a debt to Vaux-le-Vicomte and other French chateaux.

Bielke loved all things French; he may have loved them too much. The man who would later build Salsta first gained distinction as an officer in the Swedish army. On December 4, 1676, he acquitted himself so brilliantly in the battle of Lund that King Karl XI said, "Today the crown of Sweden danced on the point of Bielke's sword." Thus a great career was launched. As ambassador to France, field marshal in the army of the Holy Roman Emperor, and governor general of Swedish Pomerania, Bielke ran afoul of the jealousy of his fellows Swedes. In 1706, accused of treasonably favoring the French, he was tried and sentenced to lose his life, honor, and belongings. King Karl XII, however, granted Bielke his life and restored Salsta and Tureholm castles to him. Thereafter, the hero of Lund retired to Salsta to sulk away his remaining years among the remains of his past grandeur, which are now scattered throughout Sweden. Only the chapel, furnished by Daniel Kortz, remains as Bielke left it. It is unusual in that it is decorated with paintings of the lives and deeds of Catholic saints.

Over the doorway of the castle library, Bielke had the following verse inscribed in rather rustic French:

> *Las d'esperer et de me plaindre*
> *D'ame qui vive ni mesme de mon sort*
> *C'est icy ou i 'attends la mort*
> *Sans la desirer ni la craindre.*

(Tired of hoping and of complaining of any living soul and of my lot, it's here I await a death I neither fear nor desire.)

These bitter words seem to foreshadow the sentiments expressed in the painting of Diogenes and Alexander that Carl Gustav Tessin commissioned for Åkerö. Both men greatly enriched Sweden's artistic heritage, and both built beautiful castles in which they took refuge but not comfort when they had fallen from power.

ÖSTERBYBRUK AND LEUFSTABRUK MANORS

Österbybruk Manor.
The manor is set in a park designed by Carl Hårleman, whose original drawings for this project can be viewed at the National Museet in Stockholm. The handsome wrought iron urns decorate the property gardens, linden alleys and terraces.

These two manor houses and the small urban centers surrounding them owe their existence to the entrepreneurial genius of a single man: Louis de Geer (1587-1652). Born in Liège when what is now Belgium was under Spanish rule, de Geer later moved with his family, who were Calvinists, to Amsterdam.

In the early seventeenth century, the Dutch often served as paymasters to the Protestant princes of northern Europe, so it is not surprising to find Louis de Geer signing a loan to Sweden's King Gustav II Adolf as early as 1616. The king, extended extremely favorable terms to de Geer, hoping to entice him into setting up a Swedish armaments industry. The king's hopes were soon fulfilled; indeed, some have referred to de Geer as the Krupp of Sweden; While he and Willem de Besche were establishing ironworks in the Uppland forests to supply cannons to the royal army, the population of Stockholm stood slightly over ten thousand—not enough to supply the needed skilled workers. Hence the contract laborers sent by de Geer from Holland to man these factories were of the greatest importance to Sweden's economy, for they were all skilled.

De Geer created the towns of Leufstabruk and Österbybruk, with their small ocher-and red-roofed houses, for the hundreds of Walloon craftsmen who came for years and stayed for generations.

De Geer, who never really lived in Sweden, died in Holland, as did his sons Emmanuel, who inherited Leufsta, and Gérard, the heir to

Österby. But the manors (which in the seventeenth century were more guest houses than residences) and their adjacent ironworks remained treasured by the family, whose founder had been ennobled as "de Geer of Leufsta." Both manors were rebuilt in the eighteenth century, but Charles de Geer, the scholar and naturalist, eventually sold Österby to Claes Grill. Grill's daughter Anna Johanna Grill was responsible for the rococo building that stands in the beautiful park; it is based on a drawing by Johan Hårleman, now in Stockholm's National Museum. Österby's park is also the setting for a very handsome selection of wrought-iron vases. These reflect high degree of sophisticated

We see a fine example of a side view of Österby manor, the guest wing and the church.

workmanship attained by the town's foundries. Bruno Liljefors, the twentieth-century master of animal painting, lived and worked for several years at Österby. Charles de Geer the Younger deeply loved Leufsta. Born in 1720, he was not especially adventurous but wanted only to perpetuate in stone the wooden Carolinian manor that his father had built to replace the original house (which had been burned by the Russians in 1719). However, his interests and collections forced him, with the aid of Jean Eric Rehn, to add wings as well as whole buildings. It was also Rehn who enriched and redesigned the manor's interior in the rococo style. Charles de Geer's freestanding library, built in its own pavilion at the edge of the canal bisecting the park, is particularly lovely. It contains over 7,500 volumes. Among them there are the

Leufstabruk Manor.
Exterior view of the manor as it appears after the eighteenth-century restorations by Jean Eric Rehn.

Ortus Upplandicus Catalogue Plantarum Rariarum, and *Adonis* of Carolus Linnaeus as well as de Geer's own works on insects. Because of the humidity in these rooms, de Geer's most valuable book, Olof Rudbeck's *Book of Birds* has been replaced by a reproduction (the original is now in the University library of Uppsala). But the two rooms of the gold and white pavilion are still jammed with eighteenth-century volumes, and the guest book bears the signature of Gustav III. The twin to Leufsta's library pavilion once housed Charles de Geer's collections of minerals and insects. Today this building stands empty.

Like Österby, Leufsta's ironworks (the "bruk" in the town names) provided the manor with elaborate gates and fences, not to mention the cannons that sit graded by size on the terrace of the main building. These weapons were not meant to be used defensively but served as

The late baroque pipe organ in the church is the work of Johan Niklas Cahman and is the largest functioning organ in Sweden.

The library pavilion built on the edge of the canal that bisects Leufsta's park houses an extraordinary collection of eighteenth-century volumes assembled by the younger Charles de Geer

examples of the wares that contributed not only to the fortune of the de Geer family but also to the victories of the Swedish armies, which helped bring triumph to the Protestant cause in northern Europe.

Leufsta's town church was built in 1720 around the largest seventeenth-century organ in Sweden. This ornate piece of work by Johan Niklas Cahman is the only real decoration of this strictly rectangular room. Much has been made of the differences between the Flemish workmen and their host country; more should be said of the tolerance and understanding shown toward them by that country's monarch. As leader of the Swedish Lutherans, Gustav II Adolf never sought to convert or harass either Louis de Geer or his Calvinist workers. "No sovereign," he said, "has the power to rule and control a man's conscience."

ÖRBYHUS CASTLE

One of the most remarkable castles in the province of Uppland, Örbyhus dates from the fifteenth century. Its oldest part is a massive tower that still is the center of the building. In 1548 Gustav Vasa inherited the castle and created huge defense ramparts around it. In the seventeenth century the castle achieved its present aspect.

The gracious orangerie at Örbyhus, reflected in the garden pool, was designed and built by Carl Christoffer Gjörwell around 1830 while he was restoring the castle.

The great tower around which Örbyhus Castle is built was erected by Johan Kristersson Vasa, King Gustav Vasa's grandfather, in the mid-fifteenth century. Gustav Vasa made it his Uppland stronghold and surrounded the keep with earthworks, moats, and walls fifty-four feet high. On the king's death, the fortified tower passed to his second son, Johan Count of Finland (later King Johan III, 1537-1592) who turned it into the last prison of his unfortunate brother Erik XIV (1533-1577).

Gustav Vasa created modern Sweden, and Erik XIV was the nation's first renaissance king. Handsome and gifted with a princely sense of grandeur, he preferred exaggeration to reality. As heir to the throne, he shone in contrast to his dour father. As king, he proved changeable and dangerous. He may also have been insane. When in 1560, Erik succeeded to the throne, his half brothers Johan and Karl, duke of Södermanland (later King Karl IX, 1550-1611), were his friends. True, they had unwisely been left estates that almost equaled the crown lands in importance, so that relations between the three would have been difficult in any case, but it was Erik who made the first hostile moves.

In 1561, he had the Riksdag establish royal power over the duchies and also tried to block Johan's marriage to Katarina Jagellonica, sister of the king of Poland. When his efforts proved unsuccessful, Erik imprisoned his brother and sister-in-law in Gripsholm Castle, where their son Sigismund was born. The king then compounded this political error by freeing his prisoners and turning his attention to a vendetta

Örbyhus Castle.
Erik XIV's room in his prison apartment occupies the lower story of the medieval tower. The fireplace is from the time of the king's imprisonement and the furnishings are from a later date.

against the powerful Sture family. In a fit of rage, he murdered Nils Svantesson Sture and then ran away into the forest, where he collapsed and remained incapacitated for almost a year.

Immediately upon his return, Erik, who had proposed to almost every princess in northern Europe, married Karin Månsdotter, his low-born and beautiful mistress. In January 1568, she bore him a legitimate son; in the summer that year, Johan raised the standard of revolt against his brother. Supported by Karl and the disgruntled nobility, Johan deposed King Erik and imprisoned him—first in Gripsholm Castle, then in Vadstena Castle, and finally, in December 1574, in Örbyhus, where his living quarters are still preserved. Dark, damp, candlelit rooms at the base of the medieval tower housed Erik and his guards. (Karin Månsdotter and the children had been taken from him and sent to Finland.) Here, at the end of a stony tunnel that still functions as a castle entrance, Erik sat alone behind barred windows waiting to be freed. Despite his extravagant character, he had many supporters and there were several attempts, supported by both nobles and peasants, to liberate him. King Johan did not appreciate what he saw as threats to his throne, so—thanks to him—Erik died in agony just after midnight on February 26, 1577. The attending physician noted that the room was so cold that Erik's beard was stiff with frozen sweat and tears. Burial in the nearby parish church was surreptitious, and the common people told each other that Erik had been fed poisoned pea soup. In 1958, an autopsy revealed Erik XIV's remains to be full of arsenic.

The king's claustrophobic rooms at Örbyhus echo these grim events. Like the rest of the castle, this apartment was restored at the beginning of the twentieth century; hence the rooms' decorations are recreated rather than original. But, standing in the half light looking out at blank walls, it is not hard to imagine Erik alone and in danger, writing music, writing poetry, painting imaginary seascapes in soot, whiling away the cold, empty years. In 1643, Örbyhus was inherited by Gustaf Carlsson Banér, the governor of Västergötland. He built a baroque castle around the Vasa Tower and tore down portions of Gustav Vasa's walls to make large stone terraces encompassing the building proper. A large garden was laid out, with fountains, aqueducts, and decorative lakes mirroring the massive yellow stucco building. Cannons on the terraces spoke of Örbyhus's martial past, but the property was now a country seat. Today, Banér's coat of arms—interlaced with that of his wife—still adorns Örbyhus's east façade. In 1729, the castle passed to Charles de Geer of Leufsta, who entailed the property in favor of his nephew Charles de Geer, the scholar, and the family set about improving the property. The handsome orangerie, often used as a summer drawing room, was built in the park in 1830, during the de Geer era. In 1900, Örbyhus became the property of Eugène von Rosen, who repaired, restored, and refurbished the castle from top to bottom. The large dining room and the immense Knight's Hall reflect the taste of his generation. Von Rosen established two handsome libraries inside Örbyhus Castle, one of which holds only works in French. He also reordered and enriched the castle's impressive collection of guns, pistols, and armor, originally assembled some two hundred years earlier.

The Music room. A corner of this delightful rococo room decorated by Carl Christoffer Gjörwell with nineteenth-century engravings and family portraits.

143

STUREFORS CASTLE

Rear facade of the manor house showing its decorative reflecting pool as it stands surrounded by groves of trees on a promontory on Lake Erlången. The present castle was built for Chancellor Carl Piper in 1705 by Nicodemus Tessin the Younger.

This rather palatial castle, built on a crescent-shaped stone terrace, is situated between the southeastern Swedish forest and the waters of Lake Erlången. The present building dates from the beginning of the eighteenth century; it is the product of a collaboration between Chancellor Carl Piper, Christina Törnflycht, and their architect Nicodemus Tessin the Younger. Their plans incorporated part of the northern wing of a smaller castle that had been built in 1580 on the same site by Ture Bielke, a member of the great Rennaisance family. Bielke, having been a councilor to Johan III, was decapitated in 1600 in the nearby town of Linköping by order of King Karl IX. Ture's brother, Hogenskild, escaped the king's wrath by having his servants wall him up in Sturefor's dungeon; the hole cut to release him can still be seen today. Hogenskild's shrewdness availed him little, however, for Karl was bent on eliminating all of his competition. In 1606, therefore, Hogenskild also lost his head. But Ture Gabriel's widow, born a Sture, spared no effort to have Sturefors restored to the Bielke family. With the help of tears and pleading, she ultimately succeeded. In 1699, however, the property passed to Carl Piper. Chancellor Piper was married to Christina Törnflycht, an extraordinary woman and a wealthy heiress in her own right who improved and enriched every property she touched. Her husband, who had accompanied Karl XII on his Russian campaigns, was taken prisoner by Peter the Great at Poltava in 1709 and ultimately, in 1716, died in a Russian prison. Now the widowed Christina emulated on a somewhat more modest scale the architectural efforts of Queen Hedvig Eleonora, who had also lost her husband. Countess Piper used the same architects: Nicodemus Tessin the Younger and Carl Hårleman. It is interesting to note how she bent these artists to her will. Sturefors today stands as a severe and elegant variation on Tessin's Bernini-inspired baroque style. Tessin had planned a two-story edifice; in all probability, it was Countess Piper who insisted on a three-story building. She was ever attentive to the properties left to her by her husband, whose silver prison cup, engraved with the words "used by Count Carl Piper—for water in lieu of wine," is enshrined in Sturefors' Yellow Living Room.

At the end of her life, in 1752, Countess Piper left a magnificient estate to each of her children.

Sturefors was entailed to the descendants of her oldest daughter, who married into the Bielke family.

Christina's grandson Nils Adam Bielke was so grateful to his grandmother for her efforts that he had a commemorative temple built in the castle gardens to honor her memory. He also improved upon and completed the state rooms within the castle. Tessin the Younger had wanted to have tapestries in the large banquet hall, while Chancellor Piper had opted for linen wall panels. Nils Adam Bielke had these replaced with beautiful *trompe l'oeil* paintings planned by Jean Erik Rehn and executed by Johan Pasch. These complement Tessin's Bérain-inspired gilded ceiling marvelously. Count Bielke's study, refurbished around 1760, is a Gustavian room that was created some dozen years before King Gustav III ascended the throne. The countess' elegant blue and gold cabinet was painted by Johan Pasch in chinoiserie style, like the Chinese pavilion at Drottningholm. And the formal gardens—begun by Göran Josua Adelcrantz, the father of the

Sturefors Manor.
Chinese style pavilion set in the manor's park.

Opposite page:
The countess's Chinese Sitting Room whose decorations were designed contemporaneously with similar ones in the Chinese Pavilion at Drottningholm; they are by the same painter, Johan Pasch, and taken from engravings by Francois Boucher. The Chinese lacquer comode is fitted with antique toilet articles.

The Great Dining Hall is decorated in tromp l'oeil paintings by Johan Pasch to the design of Jean Eric Rehn that complement the Bérain style ceiling created fifty years earlier by Nicodemus Tessin the Younger.

architect of Kina—were incorporated by order of Nils Adam Bielke into an English park. This predates by many years the redesigned park around Drottningholm. Besides the monument to Christina Piper, Sturefors contains a Chinese pavilion, a gazebo, a reflecting pool, and many romantic walks. The building itself is filled to overflowing with rare furniture and handsome paintings. But the castle's particular charm stems from the fact that it is still inhabited by the Bielke family. Family photographs nestle below Brussels tapestries, and the parade sword presented to Nils Bielke by Karl XI in 1676 sits in the Yellow Room, near Lorenz Pasch's portrait of Gustav III as a child. In the castle's north wing, King Karl XI himself, painted on

horseback provides a backdrop to a prancing nineteenth-century hob-byhorse. Chinese vases are placed both above and below a French Renaissance ebony cabinet in what was once Nils Adam Bielke's bedroom.

The eighteenth-century ceramic stoves found throughout Sturefors are particularly interesting. The bill of sale for the large rectangular one, made in Stockholm to compliment Pasch's and Rehn's *trompe l'oeil* paintings in the great hall, can still be found today in the castle's archives.

A historic memento to be seen at Sturefors are the gold-embroidered armorial draperies hanging in the castle's entrance hall. These

The Library was formally a gallery and used as a study by Nils Adam Bielke after 1769 when he withdrew to private life at Sturefors. The rococo chairs are covered with their original needle-point.

were once the horse blankets used by Nils Bielke when, in 1697, he made a grand entrance into Paris as the Swedish ambassador to the court of Louis XIV. His triomph turned to ashes, but the trappings of his glory are still lovingly maintained by the eighth generation of Bielke family to occupy this beautiful residence.

ADELSNÄS MANOR

Exterior of the new manor house rebuilt in 1920 on design by I. G. Clason replacing the one torn down in the nineteenth century. The orangerie at Adelsnäs is elegantly situated in the manor's famous park.

Opposite page:
Summer drawing room at Adelsnäs.

Adelsnäs is the name of both a notable manor house and the small city surrounding it. The fate of both the manor—several times rebuilt—and the city has always been linked to the fortunes of the manor's owners. In 1781, Johan Adelswärd, who had become very wealthy in developing the local copper mines, had the name of the village surrounding his property changed from Näs to Adelsnäs. Two years later, he became master of Sweden's first barony. When the copper mines began to run out around 1900, Adelswärd's descendants opened an extremely profitable furniture factory to replace the income from the mines. In 1916, Baron Theodore Adelswärd commissioned a new manor house from I. G. Clason, then a fashionable architect, because the main part of the former building had been torn down during the nineteenth century, leaving only the wings. The new manor, completed in 1920, is a three-part asymmetrical building

whose gun room, in the lower story, is modeled on a medieval chamber in Glimmingehus, Skåne. Its library contains a valuable collection of eighteenth-century books.

The French doors of the manor's summer salon open onto a park that is among the most beautiful in Sweden, doubtless because gardens were always a particular interest of Adelswärd family. By 1782, the park had reached its present size; it has been described as containing "all that could fit within a garden enthusiast's fantasy." In 1901, the family established a horticultural school of the highest quality. Unfortunately, many of the sculptures that once adorned the park have disappeared, as have its *lusthus* and hermitage. But the garden's ornamental pool still reflects the orangerie, built in the 1860s, and a small round temple dating from 1809 still stands in a glade across the lake from the manor.

VADSTENA CASTLE

On August 23, 1521—in opposition to the Danish king who had executed Gustav Vasa's father and many other members of the nobility—Swedes from all over the nation gathered at Vadstena to offer Vasa the regency.

Vadstena, centrally located on lake Vättern, is strategically important and was the first castle in all of Sweden to fall into Gustav Vasa's hands. It stood in the middle of a town that was already famous in Swedish history, since it was here that, in the fourteenth-century, St. Birgitta had founded her order.

St. Birgitta had, in fact, held Vadstena as a gift from King Magnus before her order was officially recognized. However, she had to travel to Rome and reside there for twenty-three years before she received the pope's approval in 1370. Even then, the Birgittines, also known as the Order of Saint Saviour, were not granted complete independence but remained under the greater rule of Augustine. During her lifetime, Birgitta was allowed to found only one convent and one monastery. Before she died—in Rome at age seventy, she had completed a pilgrimage to the Holy Land.

After her death in 1373, Birgitta's daughter Katarina, in obedience to her mother's wish, helped to spread the Birgittine order to Italy, England, Germany, Spain, Denmark and Norway. Birgitta herself was canonized in 1391. In 1545, Gustav Vasa used the stones of Birgitta's abbey to enlarge his castle and to reinforce its great walls and towers. He did not abolish the abbey as an institution or destroy its church because his mother-in-law was the abess. It was at Vadstena that Gustav Vasa celebrated the Lutheran rites of his marriage to Katarina Stenbock, his second wife. The castle's elaborated portals—the work of Pierre de la Roche, a French stonemason—date from this era.

Johan III, "the builder king," revised and improved Vadstena fortifications and furnishings. It was he who added the castle's third story and built a Gothic chapel within the tower. Arendt de Roy was his architect. Johan's elaborate furnishings were destroyed by fire in 1598. Duke Karl then reconstructed the gutted castle with the help of the Dutch architect Hans Fleming, in a far simpler style. It was they who added the curved gables to Vadstena's windows.

In the middle of the seventeenth century, Jean de la Vallée redesigned the castle's central tower. But as a Sweden expanded and as canon power grew, the importance of castles such as Vadstena declined. The last royal personage to visit the castle for long periods of time was Queen Hedvig Eleonora, and even she did not stay in the castle proper but in a comfortable timber house she had built nearby for her stays at Vadstena.

After the queen's death, the castle became a granary. In the mid-eighteenth century, a damask factory was established within its walls. Then, in the nineteenth century, it became a granary again. Also during the nineteenth century, the castle's ramparts were demolished.

Work has begun on recreating these lost ramparts. The castle now houses the county archives, and a new initiative is under way to recover the furnishings the castle contained during the reign of its last great royal patron, Queen Hedvig Eleonora.

Erected by Gustav Vasa in the 1540s on Lake Vättern, the castle is protected by a moat on four large towers and three stone houses connected by defensive wall.

KOBERG CASTLE

The castle seen from one side recreated at the end of nineteenth century by Fredrik Lilljeqvist.

Opposite page:
View of the gazebo in Koberg's garden surrounded by water.

Koberg Castle was designed at the end of the nineteenth century by Frederik Lilljekvist, who also was responsible for the restoration of Gripsholm. Planned in the style of a Renaissance palace, it stands sixty meters long and includes a central tower, hanging towers, and curved gables.

The earlier manor had represented a conglomeration of styles and, in the fifteenth century, had belonged to Erik Karlsson Vasa. This background explains Lilljekvist's decision to base his design largely on Vadstena, one of Gustav Vasa's castles. The architect also faced the task of housing two great private collections: one of oriental export china and the other of books (each the largest of its kind in Sweden).

The china was collected by Niclas Sahlgren, the director of the Swedish East India Company, during the eighteenth century, when

Koberg Castle.
Hunting trophies in the hall.

The large library was built for Carl Otto Silfverschiöld and contains 20,000 volumes of Swedish literature. It has particular beautiful stoves and very ornately carved oak furnishings.

most aristocratic families ordered services bearing their coats of arms or pictures of their castles. In 1775, Sahlgren made Koberg manor into an entailed estate and arranged to house his treasures in a specially constructed gallery that runs across the central front of the building, overlooking the lovely park and gardens.

In 1776, when Sahlgren's granddaughter married Nils Silfverschiöld, she brought Koberg into his family. After her death in 1792, her husband married Charlotte Elisabeth von Essen, whose dowry included extensive agricultural lands. Thus the Koberg estate today consists of over 8,500 hectares of farm and woodland.

Gustav Otto Nils, Silfverschiöld's grandson, was also a great collector. It was he who asked Lilljekvist to create a castle capable of housing his enormous collection of books. Over 20,000 volumes of Swedish literature and 32,000 pamphlets are preserved today at Koberg in a

Part of the largest collection of Chinese export porcelain in Sweden that was gathered by Nils Sahlgren in the eighteenth century is assembled at Koberg.

long gallery covered with bookshelves and in a large library. The latter is decorated with heavily carved oak panels and contains several handsome ceramic stoves, one of which is ornamented with the bust of Silfverschiöld as sculpted by the Florentine Emilio Fiaschi. Among the precious volumes gathered by Nils Silfverschiöld during his brief life (he died at the age of twenty-eight) are the *Revelations of St. Brigitta* in the edition of 1492, Gustav Vasa's Bible, fifty other antique Bibles and Olof Rudbeck's *Atlantica*. The library, supervised by the University of Göteborg is accessible to students.

Nils Silfverschiöld did not live to see his collections installed, but his brother completed Koberg Castle to his specifications. Silfverschiöld family continues to occupy Koberg today. The present owner is married to Princess Desirée of Sweden, a sister of King Carl XVI Gustaf, the reigning monarch.

Koberg Castle.
The stables and the corner of the red painted tack room and one of the stalls.

LÄCKÖ CASTLE

Läckö Castle stands isolated on its promontory overlooking Lake Vänern, encompassing a blend of the middle ages and the seventeenth century. It stands as a monument to Magnus Gabriel De la Gardie.

Following page:
The Hall of Chivalry. Reminiscent of a renaissance gallery the coffers of the ceiling of this magnificent hall are painted with trophy groups and sculpted angels hang beneath the rondels. Two painted musicians' galleries stand on slender columns at the end of the grandious hall.

Seen from afar, Läckö Castle looks like a medieval illumination. It is set high on a cliff and surrounded on three sides by the waters of Lake Vänern; its deep moat served to protect it from invasion by land. This dream castle was extremely important strategically and, during the Middle Ages, changed hands many times before it was ceded to King Gustav Vasa in 1528. In 1617, after being passed along to various Vasas and Stures, Läckö was given by Gustav II Adolf to Jakob De la Gardie, one of his military commanders, whose brilliant conduct in the Russian wars had made the treaty of Stolbaval (1617) possible. (By this treaty, Muscovy was cut off from the Baltic and the Swedish owner-ship of the Baltic's eastern shore was assured for almost a hundred years.) De la Gardie became rich as a tax collector and married Ebba Brahe, an heiress who had been King Gustav II Adolf's first love. His son Magnus Gabriel De la Gardie did even better than his father. Councillor to both Queen Kristina and King Karl X, he married Karl X's sister Maria Euphrosyne and served Karl XI as chancellor during this monarch's minority. Karl XI had every confidence in De la Gardie, who would not have lost his dominant position had he not fol-lowed the French into war in 1674. The valor of the royal army at the battle of Lund (December 4, 1676) saved Sweden from defeat, but De la Gardie's power was broken. The most elegant noble of his genera-tion—a man given to grand gestures—De la Gardie now had the time to build up his possessions and indulge his extravagance. It was he who presented Queen Kristina with her silver throne and gave the priceless manuscript of Wulifa's *Codex Argenteus* (a Gothic translation of the Bible) to Uppsala University.

Detail of a door from the arcade in the large courtyard at Läckö designed by Franz Stimer.

De la Gardie had been improving Läckö since he inherited it in 1652. Indeed, his German builders Franz Stimer and Mathias Hall worked at Läckö for decades, as did the artists Johan Werner and Johan Hammer and the stonemason Johan Verner. The walls of the castle had been rearranged to De la Gardie's satisfaction by 1659, but a fourth story was not even planned until 1669. De la Gardie created a harmonious reception suite around the huge Knights' Hall and en-dowed the castle with a sober and beautiful chapel. Here he and all his household prayed both morning (at 5 A.M.) and evening, with high mass and morning song on Sunday. The castle's inhabitants were ex-pected to address the Lord on their master's behalf.

Läckö, with all its 248 rooms, was a world apart—a world basking in the generosity of its seventeenth-century Maecenas. Then Karl XI

163

Läckö Castle.
The Austrian coat of arms is painted on the ceiling in the Austrian salon and portraits of emperors and emperesses from the catholic league hang on the walls.

took in hand the problem of reducing the excessive land grants that his predecessors had made to the nobility. As a result, De la Gardie was stripped of almost all his possessions.

By 1680, all work at Läckö had ceased. After De la Gardie's death, the castle passed through various hands before being occupied, in 1752, by another chancellor—Carl Gustav Tessin. In a letter written to the six-year-old crown prince in July 1752, Tessin describes Läckö as being "a magnificent and venerable castle where the roof stairs and balconies present to the eye all the satisfaction which must arise from viewing, from an eminence, a sea encompassed by a Gothic shore." But as a man of the eighteenth century, he was not deeply interested in restoring the castle to the pompous glory it had known under De la Gardie. (He was already worrying about how to pay for the Bouchers, Fragonards, and Chardins that he could not stop buying). Tessin made a few essential repairs to the building while he was in charge of it, but he was happiest searching the hills and shores for fossil shells to add to his collection of natural curiosities.

Because of the "reduction," the castle's fourth floor was never completed, and Läckö today can still be called unfinished. But the Knights' Hall remains, as do the chapel, the Peace Room (where Peace and Justice embrace in John Hammer's ceiling paintings), the Austrian Room (dedicated to Austria's role in the Thirty Years' War), and rooms that await the arrival of the kings of France, England, and Poland—not to mention the grand duke of Muscovy.

All of this shows how highly Magnus Gabriel De la Gardie regarded his role as host and master of Läckö.

MARIEDAL MANOR

The weathervane at Mariedal bears the date 1666, marking the approximate time of the manor's completion. It was built by Magnus De la Gardie; quite possibly, Jean de la Vallée was the architect. This Carolinian red-painted manor house and the house at Fullerö both have the same ornamental pilasters and decorative festoons on their façades.

The artists and masons employed at Mariedal were imported from Lackö Castle, where they had already worked for De la Gardie. Johannes Hammer and Anders Lingh were among the painters employed at both places, as was the stuccoist Tessel.

There are two guardhouses by the entrance gate and two wings flanking the main entrance.

The seventeenth-century red painted Mariedal manor was built for Chancello Magnus De la Gardie.

GRIPENBERG CASTLE

The seventeenth-century yellow wooden Gripenberg castle was built for Field Marshall Carl Gustaf Wrangel.

Both Simon de la Vallée and Nicodemus Tessin the Elder are said to have participated in the design and construction of this timber hunting lodge, built for Field Marshal Carl Gustaf Wrangel. It dates from the same period as Skokloster Castle, where there are wooden models for this as well as the other Wrangel castels. In its day, Gripenberg was one of the country's largest and most imposing timber castles. It was restored in 1820, when the original ceiling was painted by Anders Björn. In 1960, the roof was replaced by a copper covering.

The property also includes eight single-story wings that are used as living quarters. storage spaces and workshops.

KALMAR CASTLE

In 1397, a medieval *castellum* witnessed the first serious attempt at Scandinavian unity (the so-called Kalmar Union). Many decades later, it was incorporated by Gustav Vasa and his sons into the fortified Renaissance palace that is Kalmar Castle today. It is built on a promontory whose ramparts bear cannons pointing out to sea and toward the town Kalmar. Secure behind its drawbridge, this stronghold was an almost impregnable seat of royal power. Kalmar, the key to southeast Sweden, fell to the Danes in 1611 but was retaken and restored by Gustav II Adolf. Its importance waned during the eighteenth century, when it became first a warehouse, then a jail, and finally—during the reign of Gustav III—a royal distillery.

This medieval castle was rebuilt by Gustav Vasa in the 1540s and is surrounded by ramparts and a moat commanding a strategic position on the Baltic Sea.

Kalmar Castle.

Entrance to the inner court—Most of the renaissance doors at Kalmar were sculpted by Roland Mackle on the island of Öland, and erected in place in 1567.

Door which leads to the church.

Kalmar's state apartments were used to store grain and, in 1810, there was a proposal to tear down the castle's walls and towers so that their building blocks might be used elsewhere. Happily, however, the Gothic revival swept Europe during the early nineteenth century and Kalmar was saved for posterity. Even more happily, there was not enough money to restore the royal apartments completely, so that only "King Erik's Chamber" fell victim to the prevailing antiquarian zeal, which also led to the alteration of the cupolas on Kalmar's towers.

Nowhere else in Sweden does the visitor feel closer to the country's Vasa era. First among the many ghosts haunting Kalmar is that of Erik XIV. Here, in the castle won (1525) and refortified by his father, Gustav Vasa, King Erik established his court (1560-1568) and invited craftsmen from far and wide to embellish his rooms. Although most of the castle's decorations date from the succeeding reign of Johan III (1568-1592), they also seem to express Erik's longing for grandeur. Indeed, in 1562 he ordered a pair of pedimented limestone doorways from Roland Mackle, a Belgian stonemason working on the island of Öland. One of these doorways leads from the courtyard to the king's staircase and the other to that of the queen. The latter, which is Kalmar's main entrance, leads up five steep flights to the castle's state apartments. Its steps are medieval tombstones which, in 1556, Gustav Vasa had removed from nearby cemeteries for this specific purpose. In the state apartments, the Golden Hall dates from the days of Gustav Vasa, but its elaborately carved ceiling was not finished until the reign of Johan III. The date 1576 is included in one of the ceiling panels, executed by Michel of Berne and Olof Anderson. Erik XIV held court at Kalmar even before his father's death. Indeed, the Kalmar years were the happiest and most brilliant (some say the most dissolute) of Erik's life. Gustav Vasa allowed his eldest son great leeway in conducting the affairs of state. When he was away fighting the Russians between 1555 and 1557, Erik supervised the nation's government. As duke and king, Erik XIV also made every effort to strengthen Sweden's international position. His famous wooing of England's Queen Elizabeth I was part of his pattern. In 1560, Erik was actually on his way to England to propose marriage to the English queen when his father's sudden death forced him to return home. Once back at Kalmar, Erik employed foreign artists, craftsmen, poets, and musicians to create a courtly ambience such as had never before been known in Sweden.

The wooden wainscoting of King Erik's Chamber was made by Urban Schultz and Marcus Ulfrum between 1555 and 1562. The room's gilded ceiling and stucco frieze date from 1585. The arms of Karl X and the date 1657 are carved above the fireplace. In the nineteenth century, F. W. Scholander oversaw a thorough restoration of this chamber, during which the frieze of 1585 was carefully refinished. Whole sections of the dado were copied in wood from illustrations in *Svecia Antiqua et Hodierna* and M. G. Anckarsvärd's *Collection of Swedish and Norwegian Views* (1830). The room's parquet floor, centered around a crowned "E," was designed by Scholander, who hoped in this way to recreate a sixteenth-century totality. But the spirit of that century can be found more easily in the almost empty audience halls, which are so sparsely furnished as to seem half finished even today. In

The church, regularly in use since it was built in 1592 was restored during Gustav II Adolf's reign being severely damaged during the Kalmar wars.

one, shadowy gray, red, and yellow murals executed by Arendt Lamprechts in 1584 spell out the story of Samson; in another, decorative red lozenges are sketched above the window seats, while the doors are framed in architectural motifs, also in red, painted on bare white stucco walls. The richly carved and painted ceilings look down upon a few huge chests and, in the Gray Hall, there is a monumental seventeenth-century bed bearing the arms of the Danish Bille and Rosencrantz families. Here the visitor feels that torches are about to be lit and tapestries about to be hung—that movable thrones will soon be installed to provide the setting for a great drama. But this drama would not be derived either from Shakespeare's *Hamlet* or from Strindberg's neorealist *Erik XIV*. Erik Gustavsson's mistakes stemmed from his own inner flaws. Although he was a golden prince, he saw himself as surrounded by enemies and lashed out against merely imagined treason. Erik's life was even more poignant than that of the historic personage he most closely resembles: Shakespeare's tragic Richard II.

Kalmar Castle.
Detail of ceiling in the Golden Hall and a nische in Rutsalen.

Opposite page:
King Erik's Room displays the grandeur the king craved, it was built for him while he was "king elect". The ceiling's coffers are ornamented with brilliant colored putti and fruit and geometric designs. The freeze showing hunting scenes with wild boars, bears and deer, were executec by Antonius Wat, the stuccoist. The walls are covered with intarsio woodwork and have been heavily restored in 1860 by F. W. Scholander.

The spirit of Gustav Vasa rules Kalmar's ramparts. Although the two seaward bastions were not finished until 1600, the castle's defense system was laid out before 1550. Gustav Vasa, and his sons after him, wanted a castle capable of resisting attack from either land or sea. In 1568, the gateway into the outer courtyard was reset at an angle, so that no one could fire directly upon the castle's defenders. The ornamental structure in Kalmar's inner courtyard, installed in 1578, was designed by Domenicus Pahr and executed by Roland Mackle; it covers a twenty-two foot well dug in 1560. Kalmar in the Vasa era was both the splendid manifestation of new-found national unity and a harsh reminder of dynastic power. Crowned lions support the Swedish coat of arms above the main entrance in the castle's outer redoubt. The arms of Norway are painted on the wall of the Gray Hall. The Vasa seal—the three crowns, the lion, the three rivers of the Göta shield—is incorporated into the Golden Hall's rich, gilded ceiling. From the cannons on the ramparts to the king's chair in the castle chapel, Kalmar stands today as a memorial to the men who created and maintained this great gray fortress when it was the key to half a kingdom.

BORGHOLM CASTLE

Ruins of Borgholm castle located on the island of Öland, in the Baltic Sea.

The first documentation of Borgholm castle is from 1281, when it was a royal fortress. Between 1572 and 1589, Johan III had the castle totally rebuilt by the brothers Johan Baptista and Dominicus Pahr, who turned it into a square fortress with a large courtyard and a round tower at each corner. In 1652, Nicodemus Tessin the Elder initiated a project to equalize the height of the building's sides.

Situated on Öland Island in the Baltic, Borgholm Castle is now a beautiful ruin surrounded by a park.

SKÅNE

Detail of the lake and a garden at Wanås.

For centuries, the rich fields of Skåne, the Southernmost part of the Nordic Peninsula, were a bone of contention between Sweden and Denmark. In the seventeenth century, Sweden prevailed and Denmark's richest province passed into Swedish hands. Although the Danes had continued to maintain serfdom, after Sweden had abolished it in 1335, the change was a mixed blessing for Skåne's inhabitants. Previously, the land-bound farmers paid their day service and rent to local landlords who, in turn, were dependent upon a monarchy in residence just across the sound. All this changed after Karl XI won and maintained Swedish authority over the province in 1676. Swedish became the official language and Stockholm became Skåne's center of government. The Danish owners fled or suffered from the "Reduction" of 1681, so that, by the turn of the eighteenth century, much prime property was available to Swedish buyers.

One of the most avid purchasers was Chancellor Carl Piper. After his death in 1716, his widow, Christina Törnflycht, was not content to play the perfect grandmother and spend her time getting Stockholm architects to refurbish the family castles. This intrepid lady, whose father had been Stockholm's greatest merchant, became an industrialist. Succeeding where others had failed, she turned the open-pit alum mines she had purchased at Andrarum into a fount of riches. Although she died in 1752, the mines continued to flourish. They reached their peak in 1766, when almost nine hundred workers were employed there. These men received their wages in privately minted coins bearing the initials CP, which were redeemable only at the company stores.

At the end of the eighteenth century, another strong-minded resident of Skåne, Rutger Maclean of Svaneholm, influenced the province's history. He came into his property in 1782, at the age of forty, and from that date onward never stopped trying to reform and improve the social and agricultural structure of his 8,500-hectare estate. Ultimately, his zeal extended to the whole Swedish nation. Maclean's tenant farmers, however, fought him every inch of the way. Having always lived in the villages, they could not see the advantage of residing on separate farms with unified plots of land. They also opposed the introduction of mass vaccination, compulsory education, and new forms of agriculture. But Maclean was more stubborn than his tenants. When he died in 1816, almost all his property was sold by his heirs to these farmers, who had grown rich because of Maclean's reforms.

The twentieth-century hostess Henriette Coyet enjoyed receiving creative people at Torup, her castle in Skåne. One of her best friends was the author and Nobel Prize winner Selma Lagerlöf. In her famous fairytale *The Wonderful Adventures of Nils*, we find a description of Skåne that presents the special qualities of the province. We see it through the eyes of a very articulate wild goose, who is leading her flock toward winter quarters on the Continent. The goslings, hatched in Lapland, have been asking what to expect. As they fly over Söder Ridge (*The whole long range of hills was clad in beech woods and turreted castles peeped out here and there*) toward the great Skåne plain (. . . *spread with grain fields with acres and acres of sugar beets . . . with little white churches . . . little beech-encircled meadow lakes each adorned by its own stately manor*), the leader goose says, *Now look down. Look carefully . . . . Thus it is in foreign lands, from the Baltic Coast all the way down to the high Alps.* Although Skåne today is irrevocably linked to Sweden, the province, along with its manors and castles, is part of lower Europe in both geography and character.

KRAPPERUP

View of Krapperup dating from the 1620s; it shows the heraldic seven-pointed stars symbolic of the Gyldenstinerna family.

Opposite page:
One of the salons; the furnishings date from 1800, though the wall decorations and stove are from the 1880s.

This prototypical estate incorporates features found in many of the castles built in Skåne when the province was under Danish domination. The main edifice, a square red-brick castle built around a courtyard, is surrounded by a moat. It has stables on one side and a large park descending to a lake on the other. Like many other noble dwellings in Skåne, Krapperup is surrounded by beech groves, but is unique in that it has a rose garden, unexcelled in southern Sweden, and a splendid multicolored rhododendron walk.

Krapperup is also of great interest for its historic connection with both the Swedish and the Danish branches of the same noble family. Built in 1570, the property passed through marriage, in 1618, into the possession of the Danish Henrik Gyldenstierna. It was he who, around

Krapperup.
Parcel gilt applique and painted mirror from the beginning of the eighteenth century.

A porcelain tray table bearing cut-out silver bowls and goblets.

1620, had the castle's park-side facade ornamented with huge seven-pointed stars, in white brick, such as those in his family's coat of arms. In 1667, Krapperup was sold to Marie Sofie De la Gardie, one of the most interesting women of the seventeenth century; she not only ran the adjoining farms but also directed coal mines on the property and in Tinkarp. In addition, she assumed responsibility for maintaining a lighthouse on a mountain jutting out into the Öresund passage to the Baltic.

Marie Sofie restored and rebuilt Krapperup, retaining Henrik's stars, with the help of Sven Rassmuson Wassander, a fortification officer turned architect. Unfortunately, she suffered financial ruin in 1694 and the property was sold in 1702. Krapperup was ultimately purchased in 1809 by the Swedish Gyllenstierna family whose arms included the same seven-pointed stars already adorning the castle's facade. They brought with them from other castles many portraits and souvenirs, all featuring the same motif. Among the most interesting of these is an extremely rare Renaissance bed that was found in London during the 1930s. It is here reunited with the portrait of its probable owner, Axel Gyldenstierna who served as the ambassador of King Erik XIV to the court of Queen Elizabeth I. At that time, this unfortunate king still had hopes of winning the "Virgin Queen's" hand, and this was also the decade of Shakespeare's birth. (Shakespeare, of course, gave minor roles to a "Rosencrantz" and a "Guildenstern" in his play *Hamlet*.) Although several Rosencranzes and a few Gyldenstiernas attended Hamlet's alma mater during the 1590s, no Shakespearean scholar seems to have thought fit to mention the grand, full-bearded diplomat who gave years of his life to a hopeless task and made his name and his country's hopes known in England.

Krapperup, like almost every other noble dwelling in Skåne, has been changed and enriched over many generations. It was first built as a gabled stronghold; wings were added in the seventeenth century, and, in the eighteenth, an interior double staircase was erected. At that time too, however, its great tower was torn down. Today Krapperup castle contains many treasures. Besides the ambassador's bed, there are family and historic portraits as well as various curiosities, including another Renaissance wedding bed, dated 1593, whose original linen bears the names and coats of arms of Axel and Karen Gyldenstierna. There is also a dark-blue salon decorated entirely with golden seven-pointed stars. But the greatest surprise is that this Swedish castle is full of Russian antiques. During the 1930s, Nils Gyllenstierna was Swedish ambassador to Moscow. These were the years when the leaders of the Soviet Union despised the past and sold off precious objects as rubbish. Thanks to this attitude, Krapperup is home to a beautiful pink glass-and-crystal chandelier allegedly from the Winter Palace, three pairs of similar but not matching girandoles, a twenty-four-candle Russian bronze chandelier, handsome Russian Empire furniture, and two huge seventeenth-century Dutch paintings of birds and animals which, instead of languishing in a Moscow warehouse or being destroyed during World War II, now grace Krapperup's double staircase.

Today Krapperup is a self-sustaining foundation devoted to local history.

SVENSTORP

Svenstorp–a charming brick manor with a single low tower and two wings of whitewashed stucco, fieldstone, and granite–was built at the end of the sixteenth century. It is distinguished by its sandstone portal, carved in 1596 by Daniel Tommisen of Malmö. The manor also enjoys the fame of having sheltered two kings in three nights. On December 4, 1676, Christian V of Denmark slept as master in a small room in Svenstorp's tower. Two nights later, Christian's rival, Karl XI of Sweden, enjoyed a victor's slumber within the tower's walls. That very day, the Battle of Lund had been won and the fate of the whole province had been decided. Contemporary portraits of both monarchs hang on opposite walls of the vaulted chamber to this day.

Svenstorp estate consists of 2,581 hectares of fertile farmland and contains the largest single field in Sweden. The clear sight lines over large, rectangular parcels of wheat and rye–punctuated only by decorative alleys of beech and linden trees–made this an ideal site for the encounter of "tin soldier" armies depending more on cavalry than on cannon. Such were the armies that fought the great and decisive Battle of Lund, which left three thousand Swedes and five thousand Danes dead on the field of honor.

Svenstorp, built in 1596 for Beate Huitfeldt by Hans von Steenwinckel, is known to be one of Sweden's most remarkable buildings in the Dutch-Danish style.

TROLLEHOLM

An aerial view of the castle built for Tage Otteson in 1538, burnt during the Skåne war in 1678, and rebuilt by Fredrik Trolle in the 1750s. It acquired its present appearance in the 1880s, when it was redesigned by Carl Johan Trolle-Bonde and the Danish architects, Ferdinand Meldahl and Albert Jensen. The castle is surrounded by a moat with a large bridge leading to the stables and a smaller one to the garden.

Opposite page:
The large library specially constructed to house Carl Johan Trolle-Bonde's collection as well as books from other libraries acquired by the family. It is made up mainly of travel, geology, history, and theology books and a large collection of old maps.

The original Trolleholm Castle, built in 1538, consisted of four wings enclosing a square courtyard. Two low towers stood at the northeast and southwest corners, and the entire building was surrounded by a moat. Having been commandeered by the Swedish crown, this castle was gutted by fire on August 12, 1678. Two years later, the property was bought by the Trolle family.

Fredrik Trolle, who was the proprietor between 1727 and 1770, did not care to reside in a red brick stronghold. Therefore, in 1750, he asked Carl Hårleman to design something more modern, and Hårleman obliged by drawing up plans for renovation. His sketches, which are quite beautiful, can be seen in the collection of the National Museum in Stockholm. Unfortunately, Count Trolle did not let Hårleman follow through but tried to do without the service of the

architect by using only local workmen. He opened an entrance toward the stables, plastered over the old west wing, and built smaller wings and low towers around the whole. Since all this crowded the old building, the result was not a success. Therefore, when Carl Johan Trolle-Bonde inherited the entailed property in 1886, he asked the Danish architects Ferdinand Meldahl and Albert Jensen to rebuild the structure as a Renaissance castle that would be worthy of the 6,337-hectare estate surrounding it. The three men worked together and designed an extremely handsome red brick structure on a royal scale. Much of the character of the original castle was recovered, and was enhanced with five tall towers. These, like the newly added dormer windows, were topped with copper roofs. The body of the main building was widened, so that the formerly cramped rooms became gracious and well-proportioned salons. Ultimately, the top story of a whole wing was equipped to house Trolle-Bonde's 45,000-volume library. Trolleholm today is an extraordinarily elegant building, proving that late-nineteenth-century romanticism need not be merely quaint but can succeed on the grandest scale.

Within the building proper there is much of interest. The first sitting room, at the head of the stairs, has wall coverings of sixteenth-century tooled and gilded leather; these were added in the 1880s. A portrait (1794) of Gustaf Trolle-Bonde, the first Bonde to own Trolleholm, hangs over the fireplace. The large salon contains an extraordinary group portrait—a large oil of Carl Bonde and his family—painted by Caspar Kenkel in 1706. The work was commissioned after Bonde's death by his widow, who had been his second

Trolleholm.
The dining room table set for a formal dinner with an Empire ormolu centerpiece.

A salon with sixteenth-century Spanish gilt leather wall decorations. Over the marble fireplace hangs a copy of C. V. von Breda's portrait of Gustav Trolle-Bonde, painted in 1794.

The Pink Salon with richly gilt rococo furniture from Italy. On the right is a painting of Carl Bonde and his family done by Caspar Kenkel in 1706.

wife. She is pictured beside him, dressed in white and leaning on his shoulder. The portraits of three sets of ancestors hang above the family group. On the far left, Bonde's first wife is pictured dressed in yellow and seated among her children.

There is a charming small library in one of the towers; its walls are covered with eighteenth-century gilded Spanish leather. Family portraits hang in the dining room, which is graced by three brass chandeliers. The one in the center was made in the seventeenth century and once hung in the "Great Church," the oldest church in Stockholm. The other two are copies made to complement the original.

The other library, the huge one that Carl Johan Trolle-Bonde had built to house his thousands of volumes, also contained his secret living quarters, a suite of three rooms that could be reached only by way of the library. These rooms now contain Trolleholm's archives. Carl Johan, the father of eleven children, died in 1912. In his last years, his suite within the library was, in effect, his home. Here he read and catalogued his vast collection of books on travel, topography, geology, and history. Here too he tranquilly studied the earth and the heavens on his celestial and terrestrial globes.

MARSVINSHOLM

This seventeenth-century twin house, originally built on pilings in a little lake in Danish-Dutch style, was totally transformed in the 1780s by Count Erik Ruuth. The gables, the two roofs, and the spires were taken down, the brick walls were covered with plaster, and a terrace was built around the castle. Ruuth was a most enterprising man who installed the first harvesting machines in Skåne. He is also remembered for creating a special cheese which is still being produced today. In the middle of the nineteenth century, Marsvinsholm was owned by Julius Edvard Stiernblad, who had the Danish architect Christian Fredrik Zwingman restore the building's original Renaissance appearance. "Marsvin" means dolphin in Danish, and the dolphin theme is carried out in the castle's door handles and decorations. At Marsvinsholm in 1805, King Gustav IV declared war on Napoleon; 140 years later, also at Marsvinsholm, an English general secretly met with a Swedish and a Danish general to plan a joint assault on the Germans towards the end of World War II.

WRAMS-GUNNARSTORP

Wrams-Gunnarstorp, which is unusual in never having been damaged by war or fire, is pleasantly situated on a sunny ridge in the Söderåsen hills, surrounded by old oak and beech forests. A red-brick castle, it was built in 1633 on medieval remains by Jørgen Vind and his wife, Ingeborg Ulfstand, in the Dutch-Danish style. The main structure surrounds a square courtyard; the nearby stables comprise three enclosing sides, with one open and leading to the manor.

The Vinds' son Holger eventually inherited the property. When Skåne became part of Sweden, however, Holger's ties to Denmark forced him to return home. He therefore sold Wrams-Gunnarstorp to his brother-in-law Christoffer Oveson Gjedde, who swore allegiance to the Swedish king.

Linnaeus visited the castle twice in 1749 and was much taken by the agricultural innovations carried out there, especially the still existant boxwood maze, the way water was led downhill to the stables and gardens, the cultivation of fish in the property's twenty-three lakes, and other improvements in the gardens and orchards.

In 1854, Rudolf Viktor Tornerhielm, then the owner, expanded and restored the manor. He enhanced the Dutch-Danish style by adding decorated gables and lantern-roofs over the towers.

The large library has a seventeenth-century grisaille ceiling showing many kinds of birds (peacocks, swans, herons, storks, eagles, pheasants, ducks, geese, partridge, ravens, and hawks) between gray and brown clouds. There is also a severe portrait of Ingeborg Ulfstand above the sandstone fireplace and a Bruxelles tapestry signed by Jacques Cordy. The dining room contains a beam ceiling (painted with flowers, birds, dogs, and rabbits) from 1636, an antique yellow and green stove, and landscape paintings by Salvator Rosa and Marcus Larson. The old kitchen is remarkable for its large collection of antique utensils.

This square castle, never destroyed by war or fire, is attached to a famous park that contains the largest and oldest boxwood maze north of the Alps. The castle was built in 1633 by Jørgen Vind and his wife Ingeborg Ulfstand in a forest of oak and beech trees.

KRAGEHOLM

Beautifully situated between lake and tall fern forest, Krageholm was originally built in the fourteenth century. It burned down in 1679 and was rebuilt at the beginning of the eighteenth century by Count Carl Piper, whose widow, Christina Törnflycht, lived there until her death in 1752.

Drawing, dated 1720, of a projected reconstruction of Krageholm.

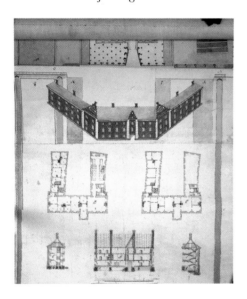

Set amid a beech forest overlooking a lake, Krageholm Castle was a favorite residence of the widowed Christina Piper. The estate had been bought in 1704 by her husband, Chancellor Carl Piper, after the earlier building had been ruined by fire. In 1707, Count Piper commissioned Nicodemus Tessin the Younger to build a new castle incorporating any still usable remains. Tessin sent his pupil Göran Josua Adelcrantz down to Skåne to take measurements on which a new castle and a baroque park could be based. The resultant drawings are preserved in the National Museum in Stockholm. When Count Piper was captured at Poltava in 1709, Christina took over the task of completing the castle. She retained Tessin as architect; it was he who designed the elegant staircase in the still existent east wing as well as the extraordinarily lovely chapel to which the staircase leads.

The chapel is a white and gold rectangle lit by round lunettes, which Tessin placed within the large, symmetrical windows of the facade. The main focus is an altarpiece of carved and gilded wood depicting the Lamb of God above the Crucifixion. It is the work of Johan Jierling, who also created the ornate alterpiece in Engsö's parish church.

Christina Piper was faithful to her artists, but Skåne was far from Stockholm, so that much of the castle's reconstruction had to be carried out by local artisans. In Christina's time, the building retained much of its earlier character: the main wing, in contrast to Tessin's severe additions, was still painted red and white in the seventeenth-century manner. However, Tessin's designs were used throughout the garden, which Carl Linnaeus saw during his visit to Skåne in 1749.

The White Chapel was designed by Nicodemus Tessin the Younger. The altarpiece, sculptures, benches, and pulpit were carved by Johan Jerling for Christina Törnflycht.

Linnaeus had nothing but praise for Countess Piper's walks and borders. Indeed, he wrote on this occasion that the whole province was "a land of Canaan" and added that "there does not exist in Sweden any region comparable to Skåne."

Christina Piper, who had property all over Sweden, seems to have agreed with the great botanist. Throughout her long life, she continued investing in Skåne and, at her death in 1752, owned almost half the province. She died in Krageholm and was buried in Engsö parish church. Each of her four children received several entailed estates, but Krageholm, which had been her particular favorite, was left to her elder son free of any liens. Carl Fredrik Piper did much to integrate the facades of Krageholm's three wings. The castle as we know it today dates from the years of his ownership. It was he who had the whole building painted pale yellow with a white trim and who remodeled much of the interior. His library is still ensconced in Krageholm; it fills an intimate chamber that has an elegant parquet floor of simple pine squares.

The house is also host to a large collection of drawings by Jean Erik Rehn, whose portrait by Roselin hangs in a ground-floor sitting room. The large portrait of Christina Piper in the east wing is a contemporary copy of the portrait at Christinehof (yet another of the lady's many castles). She is seen wearing a décolleté gray dress, an ermine-lined blue cape, and no jewels; a black widow's veil frames her powdered hair. She has a long nose, a double chin, and hazel eyes that are both alert and reflective.

SVANEHOLM

*Svaneholm Castle, originally built in
the sixteenth century, dominates the
lovely countryside around Lake
Svanesjö.*

Svaneholm was built in the 1530s by the Danish Councillor Mourids Jepsen Sparre on a little island in Lake Svansjö. Originally, it looked like a freestanding medieval stronghold with two wings and steep gables. Later, other wings were added and it turned into a square Renaissance castle. The gatehouse dates from the 1600s, as does the remarkable stucco ceiling in a south-wing bedroom.

At the end of the seventeenth-century, Axel Gyllenstierna, who had inherited the property, transformed one wing into an Italian baroque palace. He planned to make Svaneholm as grand as the royal palace in Stockholm, but his death in 1705 put an end to his projects. He did, however, succeed in creating a magnificent open staircase and having several ceilings stuccoed by Italian artists.

About a hundred years after Gyllenstierna's death, Svaneholm passed into the hands of another remarkable man, Rutger Maclean, who, however, had no interest in domestic architecture. He had Svaneholm's moat filled in, so that what had once been as islet now became part of the mainland, and he did so for purely practical reasons. As a matter of fact, it can be said that Maclean neglected the castle itself, living in only three of its rooms on the ground floor. The present library was his bedroom; the room now used to commemorate his achievements was his study; and he dined in the stone hall. Yet his ambitions were far greater than Gyllenstierna's. Not content with creating a palace, he wanted to restructure the agriculture of the whole nation and, amazingly enough, he succeeded in this. The story of the forced emancipation of Svaneholm's tenants has already been told, but it must be mentioned that Maclean went on to use his property as a model farm, first to instruct and then to convince the extremely stiff-necked Gustav IV Adolf of the advantages of modern agricultural methods. As a result, the king had, by 1807, extended his edict mandating the single-lot farm not just in Skåne but throughout most of Sweden.

Throughout his long life Maclean never stopped inventing: a new harness, a lighter plow, or a better way to irrigate a field. It is only fitting that his statue stands in Svaneholm Park and that a monument honoring him greets the visitor at the castle's entrance. But the castle itself owes its preservation and restoration to its last private owner, Carl Augustin Ehrensvärd, who modestly and carefully worked for years on behalf of Svanesholm.

When Count Ehrensvärd died in 1934, a nonprofit cooperative was formed to maintain the castle, which now contains a museum and an excellent restaurant. The cooperative, of course, was formed in memory of Rutger Maclean.

Rutger Maclean's library is kept as it was during his lifetime and is a monument to Sweden's most innovative agriculturist.

SÖVDEBORG

This is an especially handsome residence whose facade, thanks to its recessed windows, has a curiously English air. Because of its elegance, the fact that its site was once the dwelling place of warrior-prelates seems surprising. As early as 1180 Archbishop Absalon is recorded as being in residence at Sövdeborg, later a peasants' revolt forced him to flee to Denmark. Sixteenth-century documents alledge that one of his successors, Bishop Isarnus, in the fourteenth century used to yoke peasants to his plow in the place of oxen. With the coming of the Reformation, the property passed to the crown and was sold to succeeding owners.

Opposite page:
The Red Salon with its beautiful multicolored carved oak ceiling was built around 1640 for Otte Thott and his wife Jytte Gyldenstierna. Two details, one of the ceiling and one of the multicolored porcelain chandelier.

Between 1587 and 1597, Frederik Lange erected a brick castle with three right-handed wings anchored by a round tower at Sövdeborg. This is still the form of the castle today. In 1639, Sövdeborg was sold to Otte Thott (1607-1656), who was responsible for the most spectacular aspects of the castle's interior decor. He was married twice, first to Jytte Gyldenstierna and then to Dorte Rosenkrantz. The decorations of Sövdeborg's Grand Salon seem to date from the time of his first marriage, and the construction of the castle's monumental stables from that of his second.

A man of property who lived in peace and died in bed, Thott had an excellent sense of decoration. In the large Red Salon, the ceiling was covered with paintings on canvas that depict the summer sky. It is divided into fourteen fields which, in turn, are contained within cartouches of elaborately carved oak, painted in red, green, and reddish brown and highlighted in gold. The stucco ceiling of the dining room, in wedding-cake white, is even more interesting, as it is sculptured in high relief (a technical feat made possible by reinforcement with cow hair). This ceiling is, in effect, an embroidery of many panels. The lesser ones show the four elements, the six planets, and assorted mythological beasts. The main decoration, however, comprises a series of scenes from antiquity (these were inspired by a book of engravings published in Frankfurt, Germany, in 1636). The quality of the craftmanship is extraordinary; only in the National Museum at Copenhagen can pieces of similar quality be seen. The brilliance of the white, which Linnaeus remarked upon when he visited Sövdeborg, is still unfaded. But all this technical wizardry recedes to insignificance when the visitor contemplates the subjects taken from ancient history.

At the center of the ceiling, Diogenes, as at Åkerö, refuses Alexander's offer of royal favor. Around this well-known scene, Otte Thott could look up over the heads of his guests and family and observe such dramas as the decapitation of Pompey, Ptolemy presenting the Romans with Pompey's head, Aelius Regulus in a barrel of nails, Timoclecius of Thebes throwing a Scythian down a well, Crasus at the stake, Philonus and Callias fleeing before an exploding Mount Etna, Queen Tamiris dipping Cyrus' head in a barrel of blood, Emperor Valerianus serving as a Persian King's stirrup, the tower of Babel, Alexander and the high priest of Jerusalem, and Marius Curius Dantanus refusing gifts.

Scholars are at odds as to who, the artist or the patron, chose these subjects, but it must be remembered that it was Thott who commissioned the work. A strange thing about Sövdeborg's dining room is the contrast between the subject matter of the ceiling and the light, airy feeling of the room itself. The walls, papered with gilt leather, are as bright today as they were in the 1640s. At one end of the room, a large equestrian portrait shows a boyish Karl XII wearing the long curled wig that he discarded forever after the Battle of Narva (1700). In all, the dining room is as sumptuous as the Red Salon, with its gilded Gustavian furniture and its eighteenth-century porcelain chandeliers.

Otte Thott's son, Holger, swore allegiance to the Swedish crown in 1659. But since he was not trusted by Skåne's new masters, he ultimately sold Sövdeborg and retired to Denmark. In 1788, the property passed into the hands of the Piper family. In 1844, the exterior of the castle was redesigned by professor C. G. Brunius at the request of Erik Carl Piper. Both these gentlemen were enamored of the medieval and had planned to reconstruct the tower and refurnish the building's interior. Happily, their neo-Gothic projects were not realized. As a result, Sövdeborg today is the most felicitous of mixtures. The great ceilings look down on the mainly eighteenth-century furnishings of rooms whose walls are hung with paintings by artists like Lucas van Leyden, Adriaen van Ostade, Claude Lorrain, and David Teniers. The castle is filled with precious porcelains and objects of historic interest, while little black and white houses within and around the clean and well-kept moat await the visits of ducks and swans.

Opposite page:
Sövdeborg.

The dining room with its famous stucco ceiling. The doors are in the same style as those at Tidö Castle; Spanish gilded leather decorates the walls. The painting represents Karl XII as a young man.

Details of the ceiling in the dining room representing Queen Tamyris throwing Cyrus' head into a well and the fearless Timoclecius pushing one of Alexander's generals into a well.

TORUP

The location of Torup castle was chosen by Görvel Fadersdotter Sparre, who was the wife of Truid Gregersen Ulfstand and, after 1545, his widow. It was she who built the original Renaissance structure on pilings in the middle of what was then an impenetrable marsh. Torup was a truly defensive castle and—to this day—there is in it a secret passage that once led from the stables to a waterway and now leads from the library to the garden.

Although Görvel Fadersdotter, a wealthy heiress, married three times, she had only one child; Niels Ulfstand, who died at the age of fourteen. After his death, she was forced by her stepchildren to leave Torup forever. It is said that before she left she walled up, somewhere within the keep, all the riches that her son would have inherited. It is also said that her ghost roams the building, threatening terrible vengeance on anyone who might find her treasure.

A glance at Görvel Fadersdotter's portrait at Torup shows her to have been a woman capable of that and more. She died in 1605 at the age of eighty-eight.

In 1631, Torup became, through marriage, the property of Jochum Beck, Denmark's greatest landowner. In 1637, he started the alum mines at Andrarum, which were to prove highly profitable during the next century under the management of Christina Piper. For Beck, the mines spelled disaster. A stubborn man, he sold all his estates to underwrite them, but in vain. Utterly ruined, he died at Andrarum in 1689 and was only buried twenty-nine years later.

In 1647, Corfits Ulfeldt bought Torup from Jochum Beck. Widely traveled and intelligent, he spoke French, Spanish, and Italian and wrote in his diary, at the age of nineteen, *Tout le monde est une farce et se gouverne par opinion* (The whole world is a farce that is governed by opinions). He rose fast in the Danish hierarchy and married Leonore Christina, the daughter of King Christian IV and Kirsten Munk. Ulfeldt repaired Torup, and when Christian IV was succeeded by his son Fredrik III, deserted to Sweden. *Ubi bene, ibi patria* (Your homeland is where you find advantage) was another of his mottos. Ulfeldt was extremely useful to the Swedes and, in 1658, instrumental in drafting the Peace of Roshilde, which temporarily made Skåne Swedish.

Karl X showered gifts and estates upon Ulfeldt, who wanted to be named governor of Skåne. When he was passed over, he again became a turncoat and was condemned to death for this. He therefore fled to Brandenburg, where he offered the Elector of that state the Danish crown! Before he could implement his schemes, however, he died of fever. Meanwhile the Swedish king had confiscated Torup and Fredrik III of Denmark had clapped his unfortunate half-sister Leonora Christina (whose portrait hangs in Torup's library) into prison, where she remained for twenty-one years. Upon her release, the ex-princess was sent to a former nunnery, where she passed the last years of her life writing a novel and petitioning the king of Sweden for the return of her childrens' property. She died in 1698.

In 1735, Torup Castle was restored to Johan Beck-Friis, who happened to be the grandson of the castle's last two private owners. He did his best to preserve it, and his descendants lived there until the peasant revolt of 1811. In 1812, Torup was purchased by Gustaf Julius Coyet, a mysterious millionaire, who could have stepped out of

One of the best-preserved sixteenth-century castles in Skåne. Torup castle was inhabited by three remarkable women: Görvel Fadersdotter Sparre, the founder; Leonora Christina, daughter of Christian IV, who enriched the property; and Henriette Coyet, "Skåne's uncrowned queen," who wrote Torup's history.

the pages of Balzac's *Comedie Humaine*. The son of a lieutenant general and a noblewoman, he had taken his law degree at Uppsala University in 1792 and, as lawyer, had been attached to the courts of Gustav IV Adolf and Karl XIII. Throughout the Napoleonic era, Coyet criss-crossed Europe, growing richer every year "collecting lands and houses as others collect books." The Torup chronicle remarked "how he made his money is under a cloud." But make it he did, and went on to establish a tradition of lavish entertainment at Torup. Made a baron in 1815, he feasted both royalty and commoners for whom he had a dance pavilion built in Torup's park. A great gardener, he drained Görvel Fadersdotter's gloomy marsh and transformed it into an ornamental lake surrounded by a garden, which became the wonder of the neighborhood. When Gustaf Julius died in Marseilles in 1862, Torup passed into the hands of his young nephew Gustaf who, in 1884, married Henriette Cederström. After a prolonged honeymoon, the couple set about laying Görvel Fadersdotter's baleful ghost. Torup's court-yard was enclosed, and the stables were turned into a large, handsome library. The parade rooms were renewed, and many comfortable bed-rooms were created.

The first name in their guest book is that of King Oskar II. The Kaiser visited in 1899, as did Gustav V. But the Coyets did not enter-tain only royalty; scientists were also welcome, as were artists of all sorts. Prince Eugene, the king's younger brother, gave many of his paintings to his friends at Torup, who also purchased and commis-sioned works by Carl Milles and other Swedish artists. The Coyets also encouraged local handicrafts: twenty-four chairs, adorned in tradi-

Opposite page:

Torup.
The garden in which Henriette Coyet, during the early 1900s, received hundreds of guests in the course of her famous parties. It is punctuated by statues, many by Carl Milles.

Portrait of Görvel Fadersdotter Sparre.

tional gros-point embroidery, remain in the dining room today. The Coyets' summer receptions for the public grew so vast that a special branch was added to the railroad from Malmö to accomodate the crowds. Gustaf Coyet died in 1924, but his widow never ceased her enlightened hospitality. Her friendship with Selma Lagerlöf, who called her "a medieval chatelaine," began in 1929. Others have called Henriette Coyet, who died in 1941, "the uncrowned queen of Skåne."

The Red Salon furnished in Gustavian style shows decorative gold sphynxes on the sides of the sofas. The window frames contain Sergel's medallions; A Beauvais tapestry showing children playing hide-and-seek hangs above the sofa.

ÖVEDSKLOSTER

The sandstone entrance gate, crowned by eighteenth-century coat of arms, leads to the principal courtyard. This is seen in the opposite page, where the castle stands surrounded by twin wings designed by Carl Hårleman.

This castle, built on the ruins of a twelfth-century monastery, largely reflects the prodigious enthusiasm of Hans Ramel, who rebuilt it many years later. Ramel inherited the property from his father, Malte Ramel "the Rich," in 1753. The elder Ramel is said to have been a miser who kept an immense hoard of gold pieces in a locked chest in the castle cellar. From time to time, so the story goes, the younger Ramel would visit the coins and whisper, "Despair not, your redeemer liveth."

Övedskloster seen from the garden. The actual building dates from 1767; it was designed for Hans Ramel and his wife, Amalia Beata Lewenhaupt, by Carl Hårleman.

Övedskloster.

The Large Gallery with its six large windows was designed entirely by Jean Erik Rehn; the Gustavian gilded furniture is covered in red damask, and there are white Marieberg stoves with green decorations.

Övedskloster.

The furnishings of the Blue Room were designed by Jean Erik Rehn and, according to the will of Hans Ramel (1792), the room must remain intact. The portrait of Malte Ramel over the marble fireplace is by Carl Gustaf Pilo.

When Övedskloster became his, Hans Ramel set to work with a vengeance. Malte had asked several architects for projects, and his choice had fallen on Carl Hårleman and Jean Erik Rehn. After the father's death, these men were only too glad to work closely with the extravagant son. Since the castle's site was judged ordinary, the roadway leading to it was paved with stones, a mile-long alley of trees was planted, and the resulting avenue was lined with thick stone walls. The renovated main building, with its windows outlined in red sandstone, is still one of the finest examples of Hårleman's mature style. The double pavilions surrounding the courtyard represent a collaboration between the two architects, since the original idea was Hårleman's and the modifications came from Rehn. Hårleman also built the castle chapel and designed a formal garden, which was transformed into an English park during the nineteenth century.

The Gustavian sleeping alcove lined with green flower-patterned silk is framed in carved, gilded festoons; the coverlet bears the date 1651 and the initials of the owners.

The interior is richly decorated. The parade bedroom is rendered cheerful by festoons of gold flowers, torches, and ribbons surrounding the alcove containing the state bed as well as by a damask wall covering decorated with large green flowers. The coverlet on the bed displays the family crests, the initials AF-MB, and the date 1651. An amusing portrait of a dog by G. C. Pilos hangs on the wall.

The dining room walls are marbleized in the same dark colors as those of the entrance hall; the collection of family portraits is crowned by Jourdan's marvelous rendering of Silenius surrounded by the bacchantes. The Blue Salon is named for its extraordinarily handsome, complete set of gilded blue-velvet furniture. There, Pilo's portrait of Malte Ramel hangs over the fireplace.

But it is the Red Salon, also known as the Gallery, that is Övedskloster's pride and joy. This room is lit by six windows, four of which face south; it is also illuminated by two particularly beautiful Gustavian chandeliers and heated by a pair of eighteenth-century Marieberg stoves with green decorations. Here Rehn surpassed himself, contrasting pearl, white, and gold boiserie with red damask on the walls, in the draperies, and on the richly gilded furniture, also designed by the architect. It is alleged that when Gustav III saw this sumptuous room, he remarked that it was *trop royal pour un particulier*, (too royal for an ordinary person.) Hans Ramel must have felt extremely flattered, why else would he have placed his marble bust, draped in a classical toga and wearing the Great Cross of the Vasa Order, on a console between the mirrors? On the opposite wall hangs C. F. van Breda's posthumous portrait of the king.

GLIMMINGEHUS

An aerial view of this fortified castle which has preserved its original fifteenth-century aspect. It was built for admiral Jens Holgersen Ulfstand as a remarkable example of military architecture.

Glimmingehus, a fortress with walls two meters thick, was created in 1499 to the specifications of Jens Holgersen Ulfstand, its owner. (He had been governor of Gotland and later, in 1511, became admiral of the Danish realm.) The fortress which is 30 meters long, 12 meters wide, and 26 meters high and has a steep saddleback roof is a perfect example of late-medieval defensive architecture. There is a single small entrance, a well in the cellar, and a firing loft complete with gunslits as well as windows that widen inward. The building looms over the marshy meadows of the east coast of Skåne, posing a threat to all comers. It is so warlike in appearance that it was never attacked. Nor was it inhabited for long. Although it was equipped with sinks and a primitive form of central heating, this great stone mass was simply too rugged for human habitation. Jens Holgersen asked the Westphalian sculptor Adam van Duren to enrich the exterior with two gigantic figures, of which, "The Savage", has been preserved until the present day. There are also likenesses of Jens Holgersen and his two wives, one born a Brahe and the other a Trolle. Within the ladies quarters are the Crucifixion and a Madonna and Child, also by van Duren. In addition, there is a heraldic plaque showing Jens Holgersen Ulfstand with three wolf's teeth (Ulfstand) and a pole (Brahe).

Soon after the building was complete, the owner moved to more confortable quarters while the forbidding castle became a warehouse. In 1675, the Swedish crown confiscated the building from its Danish owners with a view to demolition, but this plan was abandoned after the massive walls resisted several attempts to blow them up. In 1924, the building was donated to the Swedish nation, and in 1935 and 1938 the limestone-coped moat was excavated and the old tower drawbridge located.

The very severity of its defensive architecture has helped to keep Glimmingehus intact. The modern visitor, on ascending the inner staircase, should be aware that he is surrounded by concealed ports designed for primitive muskets. These would, at one time, have covered any possible intruder, so that he could have been shot at least eight times once he had stepped through the door. It is interesting to reflect that this massive structure—made of local quartzite and carved Gotland limestone—was already an anachronism on the day it was finished. By 1499, cannon had come into use throughout Europe, making the medieval stronghold obsolete.

KRONOVALL

In 1890, Carl Gustaf Sparre, then the owner of Kronovall, asked I. G. Clason to incorporate the existing building within a Nordic vision of a French baroque chateau. The resulting construction is in its own way extremely handsome. Even as Trolleholm is a successful reinterpretation of the medieval, Kronovall stands on its own as a late-nineteenth-century variation of the style of Louis XIV. This can be seen both within and without the building itself. Clason's cream-colored castle has three towers, copper roofs, newly added wings, and—as in more southern climates—an outdoor freestanding double staircase that provides access to the new main entrance on the first floor. The reception rooms within the central building have been heightened to give them graceful proportions.

The Empire salon is a case in point. Its furniture dates from the first half of the nineteenth century, when Kronovall belonged to Raoul Hamilton. A pair of precious eighteenth-century chandeliers are reflected in the mirror over the beautiful Doric fireplace. A collection of antique French porcelains stands on consoles between the four windows which open onto the garden. All is wrapped in green rosetted silk ornamented by the rich gold and white boiserie and friezes that Clason adapted to this purpose. The room, which dates from 1890, is a distillation of an earlier period. The same can be said of the baroque topiary parterre that Clason designed for Kronovall's garden side. While seventeenth-century in feeling, it gains in elegance and importance because it is one with the castle and with the era during which the castle was created.

Opposite page:
The Empire Salon. The decor, furnishing and doors were made for Kronovall at the beginning of 1800. When the building was restored in the 1890s, the height was increased, the freezes over the doors were added and the ceiling decorated.

There has been a castle on Kronovall estate since the beginning of the sixteenth century. It is said that at one time Dorte Rosenkrantz, the widow of Otto Tott, resided here in the small, Dutch-style building that Carl Hilleström depicted in a pair of watercolors painted around 1800 and which is now part of the larger structure.

TROLLE-LJUNGBY

*Trolle-Ljungby is a seventeenth-century
castle which incorporates remains of a
medieval fortification and is surrounded
by a moat.*

Trolle-Ljungby, one of the largest entailed estates in Sweden, had given rise to legends peopled with trolls long before the Trolle-Wachtmeister family acquired the property. Two souvenirs of the supernatural—a drinking horn and a whistling pipe—are enshrined in the castle. Both are said to have been snatched or stolen from the "little people" by shrewd mortals who lived to tell the tale. One of these legends, dating from the twelfth century, says that the drinking horn was offered to a knight by a maiden whom he then decapitated, whereupon she turned into a troll. Another version of this tale places both horn and pipe at a sixteenth-century troll Christmas party held beneath a huge glacial granite boulder on the estate. When a servant of Ljungby's proprietor, Sissela Gyldenstierna (the daughter of Jens Holgersen Ulfstand of Glimmingehus), visited the rock it rose up on glittering gold columns and the subterranians tried to lure the servant into their revels, so that he might be trapped underground forever. Instead, he was able to escape with the magic objects.

Sissela's castle burned in 1525. Between 1629 and 1633, a Gyldenstierna grandson enlarged and restored the imposing red-brick building, dating and initialing his every effort. When Karl XI made Ljungby his winter quarters, he slept in what is now the billiard room, beneath a dark-blue ceiling surrounded by golden seven-pointed stars.

Linnaeus, who passed through Ljungby in 1749, remarked upon the beauty of its garden and the suitability of the estate's currants for making wine.

In 1804, when the heiress to Ljungby married Carl Axel Trolle-Wachtmeister, the property became Trolle-Ljungby. Today this stately three-sided castle, surrounded by a moat, stands in the middle of an 11,500-hectare estate. Its Great Salon, dating from 1840, occupies the entire width of the castle; in it, the royal presentation portraits of Gustav III, Gustav IV Adolf, and Karl XIII face those of Karl XV, a Bernadotte king, and Lovisa, his queen.

The library is full of rare volumes, including Gustav II Adolf's Bible. The walls of the dining room are crowded with portraits of distinguished ancestors, while those of the smoking room hold verdure tapestries. The horn and whistling pipe are displayed in a glass case, and the immense gray lichen covered relic of the ice age known as the Troll-stone has not been seen to move since Sissela Ulfstand's time.

The famous Ljungby horn and pipe have been the subject of popular traditional tales and romantic poetry.

Trolle-Ljungby.
The Grand Salon, once called the King's salon, with Gustavian gilted furniture. The three portraits here shown represent Gustav III, attributed to Lorenz Pasch, Gustav IV Adolf, by Lorenz Pasch, Karl XIII by Roselin. These were all gifts from the kings to Count Carl Axel Trolle-Wachtmeister.

VITTSKÖVLE

Vittskövle castle is surrounded by a double moat enclosing a topiary hedge. A bridge over the inner moat leads to a garden which, in turn, is enclosed by the second moat. This red-brick square castle, one of the largest in Skåne, has one tower that is crenelated while the other has a baroque copper top.

Vittskövle.

The Billiard Room; a corner showing two of four immense paintings by Gerrit van Honthorst depicting scenes from Danish history.

Opposite page:
One of the landscape paintings by Christian Laurentius Gernant.

The first known owner of Vittskövle, in 1355, was Greger Pedersen, ancestor of Niels Pedersen, who was executed in Copenhagen in 1529 during the reign of King Christian II. The castle passed through the Brahe family, to the Barnekows, who gained favor with the Danish king when, in 1612, at the Battle of Skillinge, Christian Barnekow gave his life to save his sovereign.

In 1837, having been greatly enriched by the von Aschenberg family, the castle passed to the Stjärnsward family. The building's severe courtyard gives no hint of the richness concealed beyond it. In the billiard room, for example, there are four paintings completed in 1640 by the Dutch painter Gerrit van Honthorst for King Christian IV of Denmark. The king had wanted 60 paintings and got 15, of which 12 arrived in Sweden as war booty. Originally made as medallions, they depict the coronation of King Hans, the pilgrimage of Christina I to Rottenburg, Sigurd and the dragon, and the battle between the Romans and the Cymbrians. The trompe l'oeil ceiling of the billiard room, which has smiling lions over the doorways, and the tenderly painted murals in the salon are by Christian Laurentius Gernandt, an artist of local birth (1765) who produced decorative paintings and murals for noble dwellings throughout Skåne.

In the Grand Salon the *a secco* murals are particularly notable. They are surrounded by a Pompeian frieze in white, gold, and black and include imaginary landscapes in which grays, blue, light green, and white dominate. The ceiling is covered with painted clouds and supports a large Swedish chandelier.

WANÅS

The charming multipavilioned castle begun in the fifteenth century, overlooks a large lake and is surrounded by a particularly magnificent beech forest.

This castle is situated in the middle of a large, beautiful beech forest in the region where Skåne's first cultural exchanges with the continent took place. Built in the fiftheenth century, Wanås castle is a small, unsymmetrical building that has been added to and rebuilt many times. As one approaches it today, the building looks like a red-roofed fairytale village. On the far side there is a large lake, around which exhibits of sculptures are often arranged. A rhododendron garden stands on one side of the castle while picturesque walks border the lake.

The interior is exquisitly furnished in the Gustavian and rococo styles. Besides the many family portraits, at Wanås one also finds Pehr Hilleström's pictorial recordings of the 1788 war in Finland. In one of these Gustaf Wachtmeister is depicted receiving orders from Gustav III and in another the king is shown inviting a simple soldier to sit down with him on a bench.

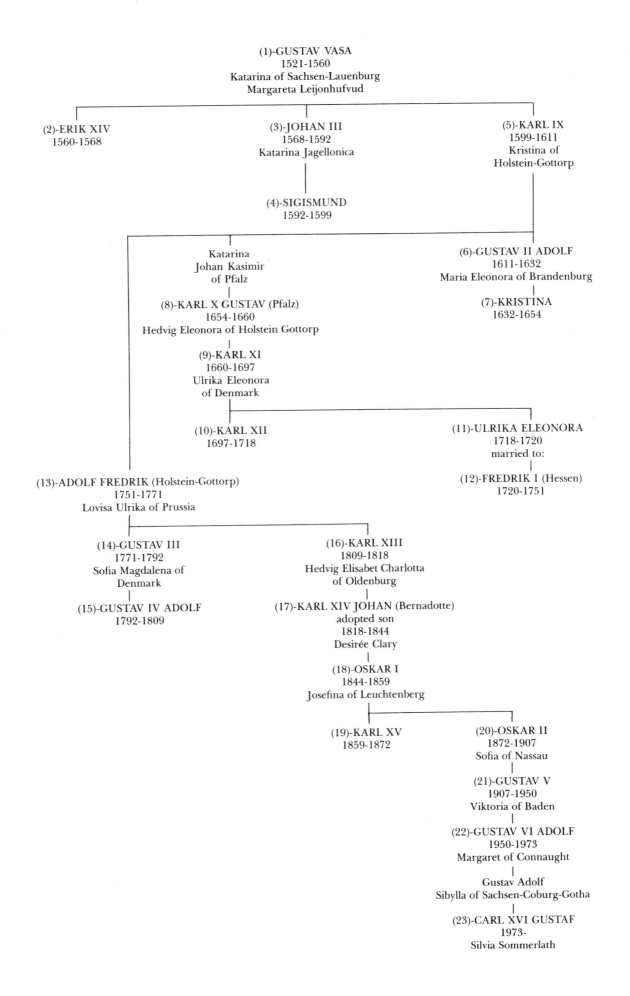

(1)-GUSTAV VASA
1521-1560
Katarina of Sachsen-Lauenburg
Margareta Leijonhufvud

(2)-ERIK XIV
1560-1568

(3)-JOHAN III
1568-1592
Katarina Jagellonica

(5)-KARL IX
1599-1611
Kristina of
Holstein-Gottorp

(4)-SIGISMUND
1592-1599

Katarina
Johan Kasimir
of Pfalz

(6)-GUSTAV II ADOLF
1611-1632
Maria Eleonora of Brandenburg

(8)-KARL X GUSTAV (Pfalz)
1654-1660
Hedvig Eleonora of Holstein Gottorp

(7)-KRISTINA
1632-1654

(9)-KARL XI
1660-1697
Ulrika Eleonora
of Denmark

(10)-KARL XII
1697-1718

(11)-ULRIKA ELEONORA
1718-1720
married to:

(13)-ADOLF FREDRIK (Holstein-Gottorp)
1751-1771
Lovisa Ulrika of Prussia

(12)-FREDRIK I (Hessen)
1720-1751

(14)-GUSTAV III
1771-1792
Sofia Magdalena of
Denmark

(16)-KARL XIII
1809-1818
Hedvig Elisabet Charlotta
of Oldenburg

(15)-GUSTAV IV ADOLF
1792-1809

(17)-KARL XIV JOHAN (Bernadotte)
adopted son
1818-1844
Desirée Clary

(18)-OSKAR I
1844-1859
Josefina of Leuchtenberg

(19)-KARL XV
1859-1872

(20)-OSKAR II
1872-1907
Sofia of Nassau

(21)-GUSTAV V
1907-1950
Viktoria of Baden

(22)-GUSTAV VI ADOLF
1950-1973
Margaret of Connaught

Gustav Adolf
Sibylla of Sachsen-Coburg-Gotha

(23)-CARL XVI GUSTAF
1973-
Silvia Sommerlath

BIBLIOGRAPHY

AHNLUND, Nils. *Gustav Adolf, the great.* Translated by Michael Roberts, Princetown, Princetown University press 1940

BLUNT, Wilfrid. *The Compleat Naturalist, a life of Linnaeus.* New York, Viking Press, 1971

CALCOTT, Wellins. *A candid disquisition of the principles and practices of the most Antient and honorable Society of free and accepted masons.* London, printed by Brother J. Dixwell A.L. 5769, A.D. 1769

COLE, Hubert. *Fouché, the unprincipled patriot.* New York, McCall 1971

EVAN, John (Simpson). *King's Masque.* New York, E.P. Dutton & Company, 1941

FAY, Bernard. *Revolution and Freemasonry.* Boston, Little, Brown & Company, 1935

FORSSEL, Nils. *Fouché, the man Napoleon feared.* New York, Frederick A. Stokes, 1928

GAULOT, Paul. *A friend of the Queen.* New York, Appleton, 1893

GULLERS, R. W. and STRANDELL, Birger. *Charles de Linné.* Stockholm, Gullers International, 1980

GUSTAV III. *Gustav III par ses lettres.* Edited by Gunnar von Proschwitz. Stockholm, Norstedts Förlag, 1986

HÄGER, Olle and VILLIUS, Hans. *Sammansväjningen.* Stockholm, Sveriges Radios Förlag, 1985

HALLENDORFF, Carl and SCHÜCK, Adolf. *History of Sweden.* Stockholm, C. E-Fritze, 1929

HEIDENSTAM, Oscar Gustaf von. *The letters of Marie Antoinette, Fersen, and Barnave.* Translated from the French by Winifred Stephens and Mrs. Wilfred Jackson. New York, Frank-Maurice 1936.

HERRMANNS, Ralph. *Slott och Herremanshus.* Borås, Prisma, 1985

LAGERLÖF, Selma. *The wonderful adventures of Nils* and *The further adventures of Nils.* (translated by Velma Swanston Howards). London, J. M. Dent, 1950.

LESTER, Ralph P. (ed). *Look to the East! A ritual of the first three degrees of masonry.* New York, Dick and Fitzgerald, 1876-1904

LINNAEUS, Carl. *Travels,* Edited by Daniel Black. London, Paul Elek, 1979.

MADARIAGA, Isabel de. *Russia in the age of Catherine the Great.* New Haven, Yale University Press, 1981

MÅRTENSON, Jan. *Drottningholm, the Palace by Lakeside.* Stockholm, Wahlström and Widstrand, 1985

PAULSSON, Thomas. *Scandinavian Architecture.* London, Leonard Hill, 1958

RIKSANTIKVARIEÄMBETET. *Byggnadsminnen.* Stockholm, Riksantikvarieämbetet and LiberFörlag, 1981

RIKSANTIKVARIEÄMBETET. *Byggnadsminnes Märken.* Stockholm, Riksantikvarieämbetet and Liberförlag,1976

SCOTT, Franklin D. *Sweden, the nation's history.* Chicago, Swedish American Historical Society and University of Minnesota Press, 1977

SCOTT, Sarah (Robinson). Pseud. August Raymond. *The History of Gustavus Ericson, King of Sweden.* London, A. Millar, 1761

SEGERSTRÖM, Sigand Loewe, Walter. *Mariefred.* Stockholm, Bokförlaget Prisma, 1986

SHAKESPEARE, William. *Hamlet* (Arden edition, edited by Harold Jenkins). London, Methune and Co., 1982

SÖDERBERG, Bent G. *Manor Houses and Royal castles in Sweden.* Alhem, Allhems Förlag, 1975

STRINDBERG, August. *The plays of Strindberg (Erick the Fourteenth).* Translated by Michael Meyer. New York, Vintage Books, 1972

TESSIN, Carl Gustav. *Letters to a young prince.* London, J. Reeves, 1755

VINCI, Leonardo da. *Notebooks,* compiled and edited by Jean Paul Richter. New York, Dover Publications, 1970

WEILBULL, Curt. *Christina of Sweden.* Göteborg, Svenska Bokförlaget, 1966

Slott och Herressäten i Sverige, 17 volumes, Malmö, Allhems Förlag, 1966-1972